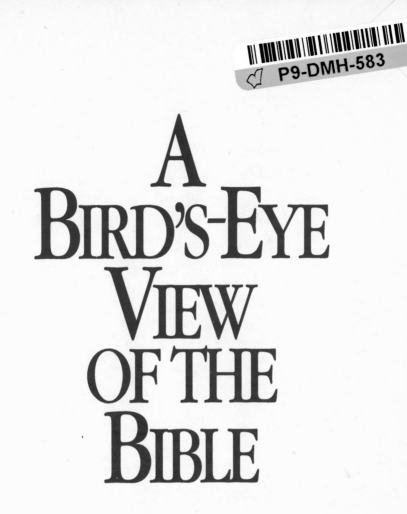

A BIRD'S-EYE VIEW OF THE BIBLE

A BIRD'S-EYE VIEW OF THE BIBLE

FROM GENESIS TO REVELATION

BETTY SHARP HAROLD

Bridge Resources
Louisville, Kentucky

Editor's Note: Bridge Resources endorses the use of inclusive language in its publications. However, to honor the life experience of Betty Sharp Harold, the King James Version forms the basis for the Scripture quoted in this book. As it is not the most accurate translation (as Mrs. Harold herself admits), we especially regret that this translation solely uses masculine language for God and humankind.

Scripture quotations, unless otherwise noted, are from *The Holy Bible: Authorized King James Version.* London and New York: William Collins Sons and Co. Ltd., 1957.

Scripture quotations marked "NEV" are from *The New English Bible.* © The Delegates of the Oxford University Press and The Syndics of the Cambridge University Press 1961, 1970. Used by permission.

Book design by Claire Calhoun
Cover design by Pip Pullen, Claire Calhoun
Edited by Beth Basham

First edition

Published by Bridge Resources
Louisville, Kentucky

PRINTED IN THE UNITED STATES OF AMERICA

96 97 98 99 00 01 02 03 04 05 — 10 9 8 7 6 5 4 3 2 1

To the memory of my husband,
Dr. H. Gordon Harold,
who was a Presbyterian minister
for more than half a century.

Contents

Foreword

*A*s conscious as I have long been of my mother's grasp of the Bible, I was unaware of her extraordinary teaching ability until the mid-1980s, when she was invited to present an abbreviated version of the course she had designated "A Bird's-Eye View of the Bible" at my home church in Boca Raton, Florida. This was prior to the first informal printing of the book in 1988, by Bill Sawtelle, a Memphis printer and Presbyterian who also taught church school. On the condition that he could use the material in his own teaching, Bill typeset the book from my mother's notes, which she had earlier organized and typed. I don't know how many copies he printed, but my mother received about 75 copies of the noncopyrighted book.

From that time until her retirement from teaching in 1993, she continued to teach the course in various locations and varying formats, often receiving an honorarium, and leaving one or more copies of the book with the church at which she taught. After her death in August of 1994, my brother David and I, having received numerous requests for the now generally unavailable book, agreed that it should be formally published.

A Bird's-Eye View of the Bible is without question a fresh and down-to-earth summary of what she called "the most exciting, rewarding, and important book in the world." As such, it deserves a wide audience, which will be made possible through this publication. I hope that the occasional undocumented ideas will not cause problems for any writers who see their words here without acknowledgment. For this reason, and to avoid any hint of commercialism, all royalties from the sale of the book will go to the Christian Children's Fund, my mother's favorite charity.

Betty Harold's Presbyterianism shines through the text, but not stridently. The book should be appreciated by anyone with a moderate to liberal Christian outlook. This was my mother's approach to her faith and to the Bible—passionate but pragmatic.

Fred Harold
May 1996

Autobiography

I was born in 1908, in Chicago, where my father was a broker on the Board of Trade. The year I was eleven, he had to go to Miami on business in February, and when he returned, he asked Mother how soon she could be ready to move to Florida—and we did. I graduated from Miami High in 1925. Florida colleges in those days did not rate very high, and our pastor recommended Maryville College, a Presbyterian college in Maryville, Tennessee. A number of my friends were going to Ward Belmont, a girl's finishing school in Nashville. I had a choice, and chose Maryville for just one reason—it had boys and Ward Belmont didn't.

I majored in English and minored in Spanish and theater. Gordon and I met when I was a sophomore and he was a senior, and we were a couple all that year. But he graduated, and I started going with the lad who played Romeo to my Juliet in the midwinter theater production. It was seven years before Gordon and I got back together.

I graduated in 1929, *cum laude*, and for the next five years was a teacher in a Miami junior high with twelve hundred students. I taught English and Spanish, and one year of public speaking, when the girl that was supposed to have taught that class dropped out at the last minute and I was the only one who had it on my certificate.

Gordon and I were married in 1934, and our first church was in Mount Holly, New Jersey, with a congregation of three hundred to four hundred. I was immediately drafted to teach the junior boys, a group with a reputation for mischief of various kinds. By then, I had five years of public school teaching under my belt and managed to cope fairly well. Each summer, Mount Holly had an interdenominational vacation Bible school of over 250, and I was active each year in that.

In 1940, we went to the Clinton Avenue Presbyterian Church in

Newark, New Jersey, and were there during the war years. It was a hard and hectic time in many ways. We had 116 service stars—nine gold ones.[1] I taught the high school class and also had an evening group of young women—many of whom were constantly worrying about husbands and boyfriends who were serving in the military. I found that teaching the Bible's relevance in that sort of situation is not easy. Also, Newark had a large Jewish population and a large Roman Catholic one, and naturally we looked at some of the scriptural background for our differences from those groups.

In 1948 we went to Pittsburgh, where the Bellefield Presbyterian Church was our wealthiest congregation and the one with the most graduate degrees. Both advantages and disadvantages came with same. We were just across the street from the University of Pittsburgh and down the hill from Carnegie Tech (now Carnegie-Mellon), so a lot of our work and a lot of my teaching was with college students. It was an interesting and challenging eight years.

The year 1956 found us in Memphis—a city whose population was at least half black, and when the Supreme Court decision on integration was less than two years old. This was exciting, frustrating, and rewarding. I taught senior highs for almost all of the fourteen years we were there and thoroughly enjoyed it, though certainly there were some tense class sessions. Somewhere along the line I acquired a modest reputation for being able to keep senior highs coming to church school and was asked to write an article for the denomination's senior high magazine, which was later reprinted in a volume on help for teachers. I really had some great students in those Memphis years—among them Ewing Johnson, Jr., son of a city editor, and now for some years on the Knoxville Planning Commission, and Brad Martin, at one time the youngest member of the Tennessee state legislature and head of the consortium that bought Proffitt's department stores.

In 1970 we retired to Maryville, Tennessee, and I joined New Providence Presbyterian Church, where I have done considerable teaching since—a couple of times for senior highs, but mainly for adults.

---

[1]*Editor's Note:* For those unfamiliar with World War II terminology, this indicates 116 church members serving in the armed forces, nine of whom died in the conflict.

While I was still in high school I began teaching the Bible to a class of kindergarten children. I shouldn't have been teaching then, of course. I remember that back then I was given a teacher's book, which provided the biblical passages and the lesson aim. On this first Sunday I was to teach, the story was about David's care of his father's flock. The aim of the lesson was to teach children to be kind to animals. I talked about how David would search for a missing lamb, climb down the cliff to rescue one, drive off wolfs and other marauders with his slingshot, and so on. I finished feeling quite well satisfied with my efforts (a condition that has prevailed very seldom in the years since) and concluded by saying, "Now, you see how good David was to those sheep. We ought always to be kind to animals."

I got a lot of smiles and nods around the circle, and then one little freckle-faced free thinker spoke up: "But, Miss Sharp, he sure wasn't very kind to them bears and wolves." From this experience, I learned a valuable lesson early on: Frequently, teaching Bible is neither simple nor predictable with any age group!

Some years back I concluded that, while many good church members had an excellent knowledge of parts of the Bible, few had a conception of its overall sweep. So I developed a course that I called "A Bird's-Eye View of the Bible." I have taught it many times—in Memphis, Maryville (at an interdenominational family week as well as a number of times at New Providence), at Second, Greystone, and Erin in Knoxville, at Independent in Birmingham, at First Presbyterian in Boca Raton—I think that's about all.

I've taught it in anything from sixteen sessions down to two (two is very unsatisfactory, twelve about average). I've also taught courses on Genesis, Matthew, Luke, John, and, most recently, the life of Christ using all four Gospels, and also Acts and the miracles of the Bible. I've also taught circle Bible study for over forty years, and in a number of years I have led classes on teaching the teachers of circle Bible study. Several times I have done workshops for presbyteries on upcoming Bible study.

I have never aspired to be either a dedicated scholar or a theologian—only a laywoman who knows the Bible pretty well, although not as well as I would like.

In a way this book just happened. Some time in the late 1960s one of the elders on the Christian education committee in our church in Memphis asked me if I would try to come up with a church school course that would be an overall view, a sort of synopsis of the Bible. He was convinced, and I agreed, that many church members, while very familiar with certain favorite passages, lack a feeling for and understanding of the book as a whole. So I told him I would try.

The Mighty Acts of God, written by Arnold Rhodes,[2] had come out a short time before, and I got a lot of help from it and from *Harper's Bible Commentary* by William Neil.[3] I taught the course that first time, I think, in sixteen sessions. It proved popular, and I was asked to teach it again. Then I was asked to teach it to senior highs. Another time I was asked to teach it to another church in the community. About then we retired and moved to Maryville. A member of a Knoxville church who had been in one of the Memphis classes asked me to teach a class for Second Presbyterian in Knoxville, and eventually I did it a number of times, mostly for Presbyterian churches, but also for other denominations and groups.

Somewhere along the line I got annoyed at myself for the mess my material was in: scribblings on the backs of envelopes, sketchy outlines, clippings, and decided if I were going to teach it anymore I had to get it in some sort of coherent shape. It never came out the same way twice, and still doesn't, and I wouldn't want it to. But, I needed something basic. So, with more self-discipline than I usually come up with, I finally produced a typed manuscript.

When Gordon and I were visiting back in Memphis, and I was teaching the course once more (this time in an abbreviated form), one of the young elders, a printer by occupation who had moved out to a suburban church and was doing considerable teaching himself, told me that if I would allow him to use my material then he would put it in printed form for me. So I said fine. Several months later, a Memphis couple visiting me in Maryville (after my husband's death) brought the galley prints for me to go over with instructions that they were to take them back to Memphis. What with this and that, I ended up with about two and a quarter hours to do the proofreading. I should have asked for a lot more time.

---

[2]*The Mighty Acts of God,* by Arnold B. Rhodes. Copyright © 1964 Marshall C. Dendy. Atlanta: John Knox Press, 1964.
[3]*Harper's Bible Commentary,* by William Neil. Copyright © 1962 by Hodder & Stoughton Ltd. New York: Harper & Row, 1962.

Because of the way this book evolved, it is faulty in the way I have or have not ascribed credits for various quotes and ideas, and I do apologize for that. I have mentioned many sources, but have very probably omitted some.

My effort is in no way intended to be a scholarly work. It is meant for lay men and women who would like to know a bit more about the Bible, but who do not have the time, material, or desire for research in depth.

I have read the Bible itself a great deal, in various translations. Each time I finish it I start over again. And I have read many commentators—from the archaeological view as well as a lot of theology. Yet, I am certainly no authority, and have no ambition to be.

There is a good deal in the Bible that I don't understand. There is some material that I find boring, some that is horrifying, and some that I wish were not included. But having said that, it is still for me the most exciting, rewarding, and important book in the world. I hope you find it so.

Betty Sharp Harold
(1908–1994)

*I*n October 1988, Betty Harold received the prestigious Zoulean Anderson[4] Award for Distinguished Service in Bible Teaching in the local church. This award is presented annually by the Church/College Council of Montreat College to a Presbyterian layperson teaching on a voluntary basis who:

Has demonstrated by active and faithful service in the local church an outstanding ability in teaching the Bible.

Exhibits knowledge of and ability to communicate the truths of both the Old and New Testaments.

Exhibits the ability to relate biblical principles to present-day living.

Demonstrates by example the validity of biblical teaching.

---

[4]Vereda Zoulean Anderson was a professor of Bible at Montreat College and retired in 1959. The Church/College Council of Montreat College established the Zoulean Anderson Award for Distinguished Service in Bible Teaching to honor Miss Anderson's long and faithful service.

Introduction

I suppose it makes sense to begin a dissertation on the Bible with some convincing reasons for studying it. Since presumably you would not have the book unless you figure that at least a sketchy biblical knowledge is important, reasons for studying it may be unnecessary to you as the reader. On the other hand, maybe Aunt Jane gave it to you for Christmas. At any rate, I am convinced that there are compelling reasons.

In the first place, I do not believe that it is possible to be really educated—or literate in the best sense—without a working knowledge of the Bible. This conviction dawned on me a good many years ago, and particularly during my career as an English teacher, when I realized how impoverished our language would be without this storehouse of vivid imagery. What would we do without the kiss of Judas, the wisdom of Solomon, the patience of Job? What could we substitute for turning the other cheek, going the second mile? Where would we find a comparable picture of the final irony of greed to that in the parable of the rich man who tore down his barns to build greater ones only to discover that same night that he was without the price of admission to the next world? How better to express the sacrifice of values and standards that we find so frightening today than by selling one's soul for thirty pieces of silver?

And if we leave the realm of words, then what about other arts? How drained of magnificent subject matter would the great artists and sculptors such as Rembrandt, Michelangelo, Da Vinci have been? How lacking the world of music, of Handel and Bach and Mozart! What about drama: *Green Pastures, J. B., Godspell, Jesus Christ Superstar?* Novels and movies, some great, some passable, some trash, but a very long list indeed are based on the stories of the Bible.

We who are Christians view the Bible, however, not primarily as a vast reservoir of cultural enrichment. We study it because it is our route of communication with God. How is any kind of communication possible with someone you do not know? It is in the pages of the Bible that we at least begin to learn what God is like. And it is also there that we find the ammunition for sharing our faith with others. We find the reasons for our faith and the imperative to share it in the Bible.

And finally, the Bible can help us cope with the world we live in. It's a scary world, sometimes, and we badly need some answers. We need some good news—the good news that God loves us as we are, now and forever, without strings or conditions. We need to also remember that there is always hope, no matter how dim or far away it may seem.

Let me make it clear from the start that I am no authority and have never pretended to be. In all the years that I have taught this and that from the Bible as the wife of the resident minister, I have always cautioned my hearers that the views I expressed are mine. Gordon and I differ widely in our interpretation of various scriptural passages (an argument over predestination, never settled, goes back as far as college days), and certainly I do not expect readers to agree with all that I say. Remember that one of the things the Reformation was all about was the right of individuals to read and interpret Scripture for themselves. My writing this book has certain advantages for many readers. Since I am not an authority I am not inclined, as assorted ministers and theologians may be, to presuppose an unrealistic amount of biblical knowledge on the part of most of the laity!

In any Bible study that I undertake, there are three things that I always hope will come through. First, the Bible is one story, not a disjointed hodgepodge. Second, its characters are real people. Third, its message is entirely relevant to our lives today. I'd like to elaborate a bit on these three things.

First, the Bible is one continued story. Too often we fragment it. Many good Christians are quite familiar with numerous favorite passages, but have no real concept of its overall theme. It simply is not possible to get the full impact of any part of the Bible without the background of the whole. There are literally hundreds of examples of this fact, but I'll settle for two.

At the time of the crucifixion you will remember that there was a great earthquake and that the veil of the temple was "rent in twain" as the King James Version tells it, or "torn in two," as *The New English Bible* reads, from the top to the bottom (Matt. 27:51). The significance of this, as of the whole meaning of atonement, will pass us by unless we have the Old Testament Levitical background of blood sacrifice and of the law that permitted only the high priests to go behind the veil of the temple only on the day of atonement. The tearing aside of this veil on Good Friday symbolized the removal of the barrier between the people and their God—access to God through Christ rather than through an earthly high priest.

As another example, how can we understand what kind of a kingdom it was that Christ's followers wanted him to bring about unless we know how the Jews revered the memory of the kingdom of David: a kingdom stretching from the Gulf of Aqabah to beyond Damascus that was both rich and powerful? If we look back to the magnificence of that day, perhaps we can sympathize a little more with the apostles' desire for the "chief seats," and perhaps we can even come to wonder whether Judas's motives for betrayal did not go beyond greed and jealousy.

Second, it is clear that the people who walk its pages were real men and women with all the hopes and fears, problems and hang-ups, loves and hates, courage and cowardice that are part of our lives today. It is noteworthy that the Bible never attempts to do a cover-up on any of its heroes. Their faults and shortcomings are laid bare in no uncertain terms. And, of course, in line with this, it gives us amazing examples of what God can do with some very inferior material.

Third, the biblical message is entirely relevant to the lives we live today. Granted, the setting is different and the customs seem strange, but the situations, the relationships, the needs and failures of people are the same. There is no human emotion, no crime, no virtue that you cannot find in the Bible. Deceit, lust, self-sacrifice, greed, anguish, love at its best and worst. It's all there. And, it makes the Bible as up-to-date as the morning newspaper.

Early in any study I believe it is important to think a little about what the Bible is not. For instance, it is not a brief written to prove the existence of God. Its authors assume God's existence. They even take it for granted. It is an astounding witness to the existence of God, but nowhere do we find the Bible accepting the burden of proof. The

Bible is neither a scientific text nor a history book, though it contains a great deal of scientific truth and a lot of history. It is not a moral and an ethical code, though it has the finest guidelines for human conduct to be found anywhere. And finally, and this, I think, is very important, the Bible is not an idol to be worshiped. A few years back I had a lengthy stay in the hospital. One day, I had on my bedside table my Bible, Sandburg's *Life of Lincoln,* and a mystery novel. The Bible was the largest of the three and on the bottom. A student nurse came by and said, "Oh-oh, Mrs. Harold. You aren't supposed to put anything on top of the Bible!" Those words caused me to reflect back to the large family Bible on the table in my grandmother's parlor, which was never, never touched except for recording births, marriages, and deaths. Hardly an incentive to a close acquaintance with the book.

On one occasion when I had finished a seminar at a large church in Knoxville, one of the participants said, "Betty, I think the reason we enjoy you so much is that you're so irreverent." Needless to say, this brought me up short. Yet the more I thought about it, the more I was convinced that on many occasions we have done the Bible in with too much reverence. We do not have to handle it with kid gloves, and I see no reason not to admit that there are parts that puzzle, trouble, bore, and even repel us. A book that has survived all that the Bible has through the centuries is not going to be thrown by any questions we can ask. *Not* asking questions about the things that disturb us in the Bible is in the same category, for me, as always making our attitude toward God pious, unquestioning, and submissive.

I don't always feel pious toward God. Do you? Many times I feel extremely rebellious, and I am constantly asking "Why?" I'm sure in my own mind that God would rather be challenged in sincerity— even railed against—than to be ignored or hypocritically praised. The Bible is no idol.

If the Bible is not any of these things, then what is it? The Bible is the word of God recorded for us. Let us never forget that Christ is the Word Incarnate. It is a witness to God's mighty acts—the one story of salvation and redemption (sorry for the theological words). It is history, poetry, drama, prophecy, letters, sermons, parables, wise sayings, allegory—all these and much more. It has been called, tongue in cheek, a collection of after-sinner speeches, and, over-sentimentally, God's love letter to me. Another author says it's the ultimate whodunit—God searching for Adam and Eve who are hiding. One o the amazing truths about it is that it is so written that the simple message of God's love can be grasped by a small child and yet it is so profound that no scholar has ever been able to answer all the questions it raises. The Bible, I truly think, provides the clues to the mysteries that surround our existence: to tell us who we really are, where we should be going, and what we should be doing, how to get there, and how to do it. Not necessarily in specifics, mind you, though there are many of those, but in overall guidelines for harmony with God, ourselves, and others.

I have two favorite definitions of the Bible, both very simple. First, it is the story of God's dealings with humankind. Second, it is the account of what God has done, is doing, and will do for humanity and its redemption. It is not a sacred fossil. It is a virile, exciting drama of life.

The word *redemption* appears above, and as it's a theological term let's go back to it, since I am set on bringing any theology that pokes its way into this opus down at least to my level. On a very easy level, to redeem means to buy back. Anyone who has left a cherished possession with a pawnbroker knows what it means. In biblical terms, what, then? I asked a young man a few years back why, when he had graduated from Duke University with a degree in physics and the offer of a good job in technology, he had all at once decided to go to Yale Divinity School. He answered that he had suddenly realized he could never make it on his own and that God was available to help him. Redemption to him was knowing that God was always there.

A great many years ago I heard a short story, used as a children's sermon, that I think offers as good an explanation of redemption as any. A little boy had painstakingly and laboriously made himself a little wooden boat. He carved it, polished it, and found a scrap of an old handkerchief to make a sail. When it was finished, his pride and joy were unbounded, and he could hardly wait to try it out. Sure enough, in a few days there was a heavy rain and the gutters ran full. He dashed out, carefully set his boat in the gutter, and ran along side jubilantly as it sped along. Too late—he saw it gathering speed and being swept into the storm sewer. He was very nearly inconsolable, but a few days later he was down in the center of town and there in the window of the general store he saw his boat. He was certain it was his and told the proprietor so. But that gentleman said he had

y-five cents to a child who had brought it in to him, and
ld have to get at least ninety cents to take care of his
the boy worked and saved, and finally, with great
...uny and sacrifice, came up with the required ninety cents. As he
left the store with the boat cradled in his arms the owner heard him
murmur, "Little boat, you're twice mine: I made you and I bought
you." Creator and Redeemer . . . created and redeemed.

Have you ever heard someone say (often piously and/or
pompously, I'm afraid), "The Bible says it; I believe it; that settles it"?
It has a nice ring to it. But it brings up the whole thorny question of
how we interpret the Bible. Reams have been written about various
methods and refinements of them. But it pretty much boils down to
two: literal interpretation and figurative or allegorical. How much of
Scripture is factual, to be taken as literal history or injunction, and
how much is figurative illustration of truth, story-telling to make a
point or teach a lesson? I think any serious Bible student is bound to
come to the conclusion that there is a lot of both.

In order to come up with a working knowledge of biblical
interpretation, we have to grapple with the concept of biblical
inspiration. If we asked a group of professing Christians how many
believed the Bible to be the inspired word of God, I expect a majority
would raise their hands, and I would be among them. But what do we
mean by the inspired word of God?

There was a time, not too far in the past, when many people
believed that the King James Version, with Jesus' words in red print,
fell from heaven neatly bound in leather. It didn't happen that way. It
was written over hundreds of years ago in Hebrew, Greek, and
Aramaic, by many different men. No women writers, as far as we
know at this point. (Sorry about that.) These writers, I believe, were
all guided and inspired by God, but not in such a way as to keep them
from using their own abilities, resources, personalities, and
sometimes their own prejudices and limitations. I don't think I've
seen it put better than in The Confession of 1967 of the United
Presbyterian Church:

> The Scriptures are not a witness among others, but the
> witness without parallel (9.27) . . . . The Scriptures, given
> under the guidance of the Holy Spirit, are nevertheless the

words of men [and women], conditioned by the language, thought forms, and literary fashions of the places and times at which they were written. They reflect views of life, history, and the cosmos which were then current (9.29) .... [(I would insert here that they also often transcend those views.)] .... [T]he church is confident that [God] will continue to speak through the Scriptures in a changing world and in every form of human culture (9.29).[1]

So much for inspiration. Back to interpretation—literal and figurative. Most of us, and most Bible scholars, take some of it one way and some of it the other. The trick, of course, is to know which is which. In this book I will undoubtedly come up with a mix that can't possibly satisfy everyone. And remember that you have every bit as much right to your interpretation as I have to mine. I must, however, admit to feeling that the person who insists that every word in the Bible must be taken literally either doesn't know the Bible very well or doesn't understand the use of language, or more likely both. For instance, a well-loved Thanksgiving hymn talks about the valleys that stand so rich with corn that they laugh and sing. Psalm 65:13 reads, "The valleys also are covered over with corn; they shout for joy, they also sing." Surely a valley that literally shouted would be a major curiosity. But we know exactly what these beautiful words mean. Christ is called the Lamb of God; he calls the Pharisees vipers. These are figurative expressions. Imagery and hyperbole have always been part of the ornamental style of writing. Remember the figures of speech you studied in English? A perfect example of hyperbole or exaggeration comes in the very last verse of the Gospel of John. "There is much else that Jesus did. If it were all to be recorded in detail, I suppose the whole world could not hold the books that would be written" (John 21:25, NEB). Even the world that John knew could contain an awful lot of books.

On the other hand, it is easy to be too quick to write off some portion of the Bible as allegorical or figurative. I can give you a personal example here. I had always believed (and for that matter, I

---

[1]From The Confession of 1967 (9.27, 9.29), in *The Constitution of the Presbyterian Church (U.S.A.), Part I, Book of Confessions.* Copyright © 1994 by the Office of the General Assembly, Presbyterian Church (U.S.A.), p. 265. Used by permission.

still do) that the book of Jonah is allegorical—a story told to teach a lesson. Consequently I never bothered much about the whale (or, to be accurate, the great fish) whether this could have happened, whether Jonah could have survived, and so on. However, back in the late 1930s, off the coast of Florida, a huge whale beached itself. This does sometimes happen. The creature was unable to get back into the ocean. So the SPCA, the city government, and what not tried everything in their power—winches, pulleys, and the like—to move it down to the water. They failed, and after a couple days the whale died. Then there was a sanitation problem. Crews began to cut up the huge carcass into manageable hunks. And, in the interior of that whale, they found a twelve-hundred-pound sea creature (I remember the weight, but not the name) still alive. So then I wondered if I were as smart as I had thought.

The tragedy in too much argument about interpretation is that often it misses the whole point of the passage under debate. Jonah, for instance, is not a book about a whale at all—it is a stinging rebuke to prejudice and narrow-minded nationalism, as we will see when we get there.

What can I say, then, as advice on interpretation? Well, use your common sense, a good commentary, and prayer. And remember, that one of the things the Reformation was all about was the right of the individual to read and interpret Scripture for himself or herself. Don't miss the real message because you aren't sure whether to take something literally or figuratively. And, good luck!

Now, are we ready to look at the book itself? Not quite. I think we need to ask one more question: How reliable is this record, this composite of widely different books that finally made it into the canon? By canon we mean today the compilation of books that were accepted into the Old and New Testaments, the former around the end of the first century, perhaps C.E. 90 and the New Testament not in its present form until the fourth or perhaps early fifth century. The very fact that it took so long and that it was so difficult for some books to get in is a testimony to the reliability of the contents of the whole. This assembling of the canon is a fascinating study, but has no place in a book of this sort, except as one indication of trustworthiness.

Another, of course, comes from archaeology. Archaeology again and again has shown with what faithfulness the biblical writers recorded contemporary events. All of us are intrigued by new discoveries—recent excavations of Nineveh, of Solomon's stables and the like—which reinforce biblical accounts. One of the most exciting events in modern times was the discovery of the Dead Sea Scrolls, and one of the most interesting facts connected with that discovery was that in scroll after scroll material already in the Bible was simply repeated—reinforced, as it were. Albert Schweitzer, renowned scholar and radical Bible critic, though a devout Christian, said in his *Quest of the Historical Jesus,*

> When we have once made up our minds that we have not the materials for a complete Life of Jesus, but only for a picture of His public ministry, it must be admitted that there are few characters of antiquity about whom we possess so much indubitably historical information, of whom we have so many authentic, discourses. The position is much more favourable, for instance, than in the case of Socrates; for he is pictured to us by literary men who exercised their creative ability upon the portrait. Jesus stands much more immediately before us, because He was depicted by simple Christians without literary gift.[2]

The final reason, of course, for believing the Bible is a reason of faith and faith is its own justification. So then—to our bird's-eye view.

---

[2]From *The Quest of the Historical Jesus,* by Albert Schweitzer. New York: The Macmillan Company, 1948, p. 6.

2

Prologue

*I*n *Harper's Bible Commentary,* William Neil, one of my favorite modern commentators, chooses to look at the Bible as a drama, with a prologue, three acts, and an epilogue. While this is overly simplistic, by and large it is a useful gimmick. Neil sees the first eleven chapters of Genesis (up to the call of Abraham) as prologue; the remainder of the Old Testament as Act 1; the gospels as Act 2; the book of Acts as Act 3; and the epilogue as Revelation.[1]

Certainly Genesis 1:1 to 11:9 constitute a different sort of record than the rest of the Bible. This is what I call the prehistoric part of the Bible—ancient accounts handed down, by word of mouth, from one generation to the next, back in the mists of time before there were any written records. Some scholars call these the myths of the Bible, which is all too likely to get some people's backs up because they do not understand the meaning of the word *myth* as used in this sense. A myth is a story told to illustrate a great truth. But, it is more in that somehow it grows out of the experience of a people. The events cataloged in Genesis's first eleven chapters cannot be set into any historical frame, nor can any approximate dates be assigned, nor is there any setting apart from a race of people. All this changes when Abraham comes on the scene.

What, then, is encompassed in the prologue? Two stories of the Creation are there, along with the temptation and the Fall. Cain and Abel, Adam and his descendants, Noah and the Flood and his descendants, and finally, the Tower of Babel are also found there. This material was not put into its present form until somewhere between 500 and 300 B.C.E.

I think it's always important to remember that biblical dates are highly debatable, especially for the Old Testament. However, I think

---

[1]See *Harper's Bible Commentary,* by William Neil. Copyright © 1962 by Hodder & Stoughton Ltd. New York: Harper & Row, 1962, p. 13.

approximate dates are helpful, even though attempts to pinpoint them usually lead to argument, particularly when a couple of ardent scholars are involved, and as I've already said, I have never aspired to be an ardent scholar.

The priestly editors had at least three ancient documents to draw from (designated by scholars J, E, and P, in order of their antiquity) as well as valid traditions much older. Incidentally, in my studying, I've read in various sources that there are in existence more than two thousand Hebrew and fifteen hundred Greek Old Testament manuscripts, and over five thousand Greek New Testament ones. For comparison, there are about one hundred manuscripts of Homer's *Odyssey.*

The use of more than one record shows clearly in the Creation stories since there are two of them. In the first chapter we find, "So God created man in his *own* image, . . . male and female created he them" (v. 27). In the second chapter we find, "And the Lord God formed man *of* the dust of the ground" (v. 7), and "the rib, which the Lord God had taken from man, made he a woman" (v. 22).

What about the Creation stories? Nowhere is the argument over literal/figurative interpretation more volatile than here. Did God make the world and its inhabitants in six 24-hour days? You can still find people, though not as many as some years back, who feel that it is blasphemous to take any other view. My own feeling is that certainly God could have done it that way if he had so chosen. But, if he had, then the God I worship would never have left all the misleading evidence that it took millions of years.

How, then, do we reconcile this? There are many ways. One is that the Hebrew word for day really means a measured length of time and can be translated to mean "era" as well as "day." Another explanation is that in between Genesis 1:1 and 1:2, millions of years could have gone by. The Bible is frequently casual about the passing of time. For example, the length of time between Paul's conversion and his acceptance by the apostles; and also note the psalmist's words, "For a thousand years in thy sight *are but* as yesterday when it is past, and *as* a watch in the night" (Ps. 90:4).

These origin stories are not historical in the ordinary sense, since by their very nature they lie beyond the possibility of historical verification. They convey great and magnificent truths: that God is the creator, and that all that was created is good.

Robert Ingersoll was a well-known atheist and favored a view of creation by accident or spontaneous combustion. One day he was visiting an astromer friend, who was a Christian, and admiring his latest acquisition, a beautiful model of the universe, of crystal, platinum wire, etc., he was said to exclaim, "This is exquisite—who made it? And the friend replied, tongue in cheek, "Oh, nobody made it—it just happened."

Perhaps the most important words in the entire Old Testament are the four with which it opens: "In the beginning God . . . ."

When we come to God's creation of humankind, the question usually arises as to whether Adam and Eve were actual individuals or whether they are to be taken as types—as representatives of humanity. I might point out that the Hebrew word for "Adam" can be translated as mankind and that "Eve" means woman or mother of all living. But does it really matter? The impact of the story is the same, the truth as clear regardless of how we take these early chapters. God the Creator. Humankind the creature.

By the third chapter of Genesis, we are already moving away from the condition of all being good. God has given to Adam and Eve a beautiful garden to enjoy with one prohibition only—there is one fruit of the tree in the midst of the garden which they are forbidden to eat. Evil enters the garden in the form of a serpent. Where did evil come from? Is all evil of humankind's own making, or is it a separate force? Did God create evil? Why does God permit it?

These questions have plagued humanity—scholar, theologian, peasant, rebel—throughout the centuries. At any rate, sin enters the garden. Eve allows herself to be persuaded to disobedience by the serpent, and then Adam becomes involved. It is not really much fun sinning alone.

I remember an account of the Fall given by a minister's four-year-old son reporting on his Sunday school lesson to his mother: "There was this big ole worm, and he says to the lady, 'Hi, lady, have an apple?' and the lady says, 'Nope, can't eat apples,' and the worm says, 'Aw, look how pretty it is—have just a bite.' And the lady says, 'Aw pshaw . . . don't care if I do.' "

So, here is sin. An act of disobedience—an attitude of rebellion. There is a shifting of responsibility for the act, in particular Adam's alibi alluding to what's happened as probably being all God's fault: "The woman whom thou gavest *to be* with me, she gave me of the tree, and I did eat" (3:12). Eve blamed the serpent: "The serpent beguiled me, and I did eat" (v. 13).

What is sin, anyway? Certainly both act and attitude. Some of you will remember in The Shorter Catechism the answer to what is sin: "Sin is any want of conformity unto, or transgression of, the law of God" (7.014).[2] Indeed it is. But surely there is an easier way to say it. My own rather unorthodox definition is that sin is whatever separates us from God and from our fellow humans. What is perhaps clearer than a definition of sin is the picture of its consequences. Here in the garden so long ago, and surely in our lives today, sin results in broken relationships—in separation. Apparently that earliest relationship between God and these two humans had been one of openness, trust, and fellowship. I love the picture of hearing "the voice of the LORD God walking in the garden in the cool of the day" (3:8). But on this day, Adam and Eve hid. They lose the garden of innocence and trust, and ever since, God and God's creation have both been struggling to find that early relationship again.

Once more from The Shorter Catechism: "What is the chief end of [humankind]? [Humankind's] chief end is to glorify God, and to enjoy [God] forever" (7.001).[3]

By the fourth chapter of Genesis the broken relationship between humankind and God extends to brokenness between human and human for here we have the story of Cain and Abel, one filled with pride, jealousy, murder, and grief. Adam and Eve lose both of their sons, with Abel dead and Cain a fugitive. A third son, Seth, becomes their comfort.

Because this is intended as a brief overall view, I must resist the temptation of following byways and going into too much detail. By the sixth chapter, many generations have lived and died. Here, the Scripture tells us that "the wickedness of man *was* great in the earth" (v. 5) and "it repented the LORD that he had made man on the earth, and it grieved him at his heart" (v. 6). What sad, sad verses!

---

[2]From *The Constitution of the Presbyterian Church (U.S.A.), Part I, Book of Confessions.* Copyright © 1994 by the Office of the General Assembly, p. 182. Used with permission.

[3]From *The Constitution of the Presbyterian Church (U.S.A.), Part I, Book of Confessions,* p. 181. Used with permission.

I might insert here that I am using the King James Version for most of my quotes simply because it is the one with which I am most familiar and for which for my ear has the most music. There are many excellent versions that I use for study and for reference and I hope there will be many more. It is very exciting to find, from another translation, a new slant on a well-known story or verse.

Going back for a moment to Cain and Abel, to the question that God asked Cain (and Cain's answer): "Where *is* Abel thy brother?" "I know not: *Am* I my brother's keeper?" (4:9). Certainly these two queries still plague us today. Why must I bother about those less fortunate than I, and why must I bother particularly when their misfortunes are largely their own fault, that is, through laziness, indifference, and the like? One reason, certainly, is implicit in Dwight L. Moody's statement on looking at a bum in the gutter: "There, but for the grace of God, go I."[4] If that question about being our neighbors' keepers had been answered in the affirmative down through the ages, what a different world we might have today!

But it wasn't that way. By the time of Noah, humankind's sins are so great that God is ready to write off the whole thing if it had not been for one righteous family. So we have the story of the Flood: Noah's faith in following God's orders; the appalling watery destruction; God's means of saving a remnant—a part of humanity, along with the other living things of creation. Here again, we could spend a lot of time arguing over how literally we are to take the story. It is worth pointing out that in every Eastern culture there is a legend of a great flood and that there is archaeological evidence that water covered a great part of Mesopotamia in early times. Of recent years, there has been a good deal of talk about the possibility that the ark itself still exists frozen in the ice about eighteen thousand feet up on the side of Mount Ararat, on the border between Turkey and Russia. Some fairly prestigious scientists have made journeys to look and have claimed that a piece of wood found in that general area and carbon-dated can be assigned to around 4000 B.C.E. Other scientists are in

---

[4]Origin of this quotation is credited to John Bradford, c. 1510-55, an English Protestant martyr, who, on seeing a group of criminals being led to their execution, said, "But for the grace of God there goes John Bradford." From *The Oxford Dictionary of Quotations.* Fourth Edition. Copyright © Oxford University Press, 1979, 1992. New York: Oxford University Press, 1992, p. 139. Used by permission.

disagreement. If we want to take the ark story literally, then certainly we must admit that the housekeeping difficulties boggle the mind.

I can't resist including a few gems concerning this story from Sunday school students I've taught:

"What was the name of Noah's wife? Joan of Ark, of course."

Madeline L'Engle has a delightful soliloquy by Mrs. Noah, in which she laments Noah's ability to get away from it all by retiring to the hold with a skinful of wine . . and then coming to bed smelling of "armadillo dung and platypus piss."

The Flood, whether we take it literally or allegorically, is the symbol of God's judgment of us as we are—twentieth-century humanity no less than ancient humanity. Extinction is what we deserve—what humankind has always deserved. But God's grace saves us.

After the Flood we hear for the first time of a covenant—a very important word in the Bible. A covenant involves an agreement and a relationship between the Creator and creation, and in this first covenant, Genesis 8:21-22 and Genesis 9:12-13, God promises us an orderly universe, a world we can depend upon. Genesis 8:22 reads, "While the earth remaineth, seedtime and harvest, and cold and heat, summer and winter, and day and night shall not cease."

The last story in the prologue is of the Tower of Babel. "Babel" is the word for Babylon, all through the Bible a symbol for wickedness. What happens? In a nutshell, civilization advances; a city is built; this city is crowned with a tower, probably a ziggurat, a stepped tower like a pyramid. The pride, arrogance, and self-sufficiency bring about not only a confusion of tongues so that the people can no longer understand each other, but also a deep disharmony that blocks unity and prevents the people from being community. Does this sound extremely ancient? Or does it sound very much like some of what is happening today with our almost unbelievable technological advances and at the same time our inability to solve problems of poverty, starvation, pollution, and the like?

3

Abraham, Isaac, Jacob, and Joseph: The Patriarchs

We come now, in the latter part of the genealogy in the eleventh chapter of Genesis, to the first mention of Abram. Here begins the historical record of the Bible. From here on we can set very approximate dates, always remembering that scholars disagree over almost any Old Testament date. We can say that Abram comes on the scene at around 2000 B.C.E., about as far on the other side of Christ as we are on this side, give or take a quarter century. Adam, Eve, Noah, and their progeny were not Jew or Gentile, but types of a wider humanity. With Abram we get a race set apart—the Jews, the chosen people of God.

You may have asked, Why the Jews? A little couplet says it well: "How odd/ of God/ to choose/ the Jews!"[1] The catch, of course, was that these people were chosen for purpose rather than privilege, which was always hard for the Hebrews to understand and remember. We are not very different in our attitude, are we? As Christians, we are God's chosen people. We fall into the same trap of wanting always to claim the privileges, but all too willing to shirk the responsibilities. This comes through clearly in the question heard so often: "Why did this happen to me? I'm a good Christian. I go to church, contribute time and money"—as if being a Christian were some inexpensive type of calamity insurance.

So Abram, called by God to leave his home in Ur of the Chaldees (present day Iraq), goes to Canaan—the land of promise. God tells Abram that he shall be the founder of a great nation. Even back this far, God warns that his grace and love are not only for the Jews, but for all. In Genesis 12:3 we read these words the Lord said to Abram: ". . . in thee shall all families of the earth be blessed."

What sort of person was Abram? What were the members of his

---

[1] Origin of couplet unknown.

family and the servants like? The Near East in their day had already seen some highly developed civilizations with written records, irrigation systems, commerce, art, literature, mighty empires. In archaeological terms this period is known as the Middle Bronze Age. Abram and his family were nomads, so they were comparatively primitive Semites.

Abram was a desert sheik without, certainly, the education and advantages of, for example, the ruling house in the Egypt of that day. The one thing that these Semitic wanderers had, possessed by no other people of their day, was a concept of one God who was in all ways immeasurably above all creation. The gods of other cultures of the day were numerous and usually prey to all the human failings.

Abram (later at God's decree called Abraham, the father of the Hebrew nation) had amazing qualities of faith, trust, and daring. These came through especially in two major events of his life. The first, mentioned above, was his obedience to God's command to leave the land that he knew, in order to go "unto a land that I will show thee" (Gen. 12:1). This couldn't have been an easy decision, but as far as the record shows he did not hesitate. Abram had been promised that his descendants would be many, but the years go by and there is no child. In time, he and Sarai become so desperate that Abram fathers a child by Sarai's handmaid, Hagar, and the boy is called Ishmael. This was a fairly accepted custom in that time and place. Finally, long after Abraham and Sarah believed it could happen, Sarah becomes pregnant and Isaac is born. There is again a mention of a covenant, and its sign is to be the circumcision of the male child.

When Isaac is a half-grown lad, Abraham is told to give him as a sacrifice to Jehovah. What a frightful demand! Unbelievable to our modern ears! Not quite so unthinkable during Abraham's day, since human sacrifice, including child sacrifice, was practiced. But even so, this was the long-awaited son of the promise—the bearer of the covenant. How could Abraham even contemplate such an act? Apparently his faith in God was so great he believed that if necessary to fulfill the promise, God could and would raise Isaac from the dead (Heb. 11:19).

You know the conclusion to this dramatic story, of course. As Abraham prepared to slay his son, an angel of the Lord called to him saying, "Lay not thine hand upon the lad, neither do thou any thing unto him" (Gen. 22:12). Then Abraham lifts his eyes and sees a ram caught in a thicket, the substitute for Isaac. What the emotions of both father and son must have been on that long ago morning!

The story goes on. Sarah dies and Isaac is married to Rebekah, a cousin. Although the two have not met until just before the marriage, it is a love match. Isaac was no doubt a good and God-fearing man. However, he seems, in comparison with his father and with his sons, a somewhat colorless character. Not so the twin sons born to him and Rebekah: Esau, the elder by a few minutes, and Jacob, the younger. In those days and in that place, it was a tremendous advantage to be the elder son because the elder one inherited most of the goodies. I can well imagine Jacob's indignant feeling that a quarter of an hour shouldn't make such a drastic difference in his life. So he cheats his brother—twice.

Jacob is a prime example of the Bible's refusal to gloss over any of its heroes, and Jacob comes through as a cheat, a liar, and a coward. Yet it is through him that the covenant promise will run. How encouraging we should find it that God is able to do so much with very inferior material! You remember, in Sunday school in your early days, the story of Esau's selling his birthright for a mess of pottage (likely a bowl of lentil stew). He has come in from hunting and finds Jacob, a stay at-home son and mother's pet, cooking at the stove. I am not sure whether Jacob's hard bargain or Esau's holding so lightly his birthright was more reprehensible. When they are grown, Jacob and his mother plot to deceive Isaac, who by now is old and almost blind. In Genesis 27, we read that Jacob and his mother, Rebekah, convince Isaac that Jacob is in fact Esau, and Isaac gives to Jacob the ritual blessing due the eldest son. When Esau finds out about all this, he becomes so angered that he is ready to kill his brother. So, Jacob flees into the desert empty-handed, back toward his mother's old home. That first night, he has a dream about a ladder reaching to heaven, the inspiration for the well-loved spiritual: "We are climbing Jacob's ladder." Here, I believe, a change begins in Jacob, for he feels the presence of God, and it is here that he makes a promise. Actually, of course, he is bargaining with God.

Do you ever find yourself doing this? If only God will let such a thing happen, or not happen, then we will be more diligent in our Bible study, more faithful at prayer, more considerate of others, and so on. Within Jacob's promise, incidentally, in Genesis 28:20–22 we find the first mention of the tithe.

Jacob arrives at his uncle Laban's, who has two daughters, and he falls in love with Rachel, the younger, at first sight. Jacob offers seven years of service for her, and these years seemed unto him "*but* a few days, for the love he had to her" (Gen. 29:20). After the seven years, Jacob finds that in Laban he has met his match in trickery, for once the marriage with his heavily veiled wife has been consummated, he discovers that he has in fact wedded Leah, the elder daughter, since according to Laban, "It must not be so done in our country, to give the younger before the firstborn" (29:26). However, Laban, with an eye always to his own advantage, says that Jacob can have Rachel as well for seven more years of servitude, though he needn't wait to take her as wife.

Poor Leah. She is the loser in the whole deal, yet a winner, too. She bears Jacob four sons while Rachel is childless. This was a great reproach for a woman, so Rachel sends her maid to her husband and two more sons are added to the growing list. Leah is not about to surrender any of her advantages, so she sends her maid to Jacob with two more boys as the result and all this with long hard days in the fields and desert as well! What a busy lad our Jacob must have been!

After a considerable length of time, Leah has two more sons. Then at long last Rachel's prayers are heard, and Joseph is born, the eleventh boy in the family, and all of these within the second seven years of Jacob's servitude.

Now Jacob is ready to head for home. But, Laban is loath to lose a good worker, who obviously enjoys the favor of God (Gen. 30:27). For a certain share of the flocks in his care, Jacob stays another six years, and so skillful is his breeding technique that in that short space of time he becomes a wealthy man. Now he is ready to return to his father's house, hoping that time has blunted the edge of Esau's anger. Because the two tricksters, Jacob and Laban, cannot trust each other, they want God to see that neither gets the advantage, and this, as ironic as it may seem, is where we get the beautiful Mizpah benediction: "The LORD watch between me and thee, when we are absent one from another" (Gen. 31:49).

On his way home, Jacob again encounters God, or God's representative. Jacob wrestles with the being. His name becomes

Israel, and again he changes and becomes a little more as God intends. He and Esau are reconciled. Jacob buys land and settles down in Canaan. Rachel has a second son, Benjamin, and she dies in childbirth. Isaac dies (after a very long old age, since he was old when Jacob had fled twenty years before).

Jacob's twelve sons and their progeny fulfill the promise made to Abraham that his seed will become a great nation. For it is from these twelve that the twelve tribes of the Israelites spring. The line of the story, however, goes through Joseph, the first son of the beloved Rachel. He is his father's favorite. Jacob makes no secret of his preference for Joseph, which sets up an unhappy situation, for his brothers are exceedingly jealous. Joseph undoubtedly grows up spoiled and makes relationships no better by regaling his siblings with accounts of his dreams that imply he is to be the top banana. Their hatred grows and one day it boils over. You remember the story: He is sold as a slave; Jacob is told that his son Joseph is dead, and his grief is overwhelming (Gen. 37:19ff).

The story shifts to Egypt, where Joseph is bought by a captain of the pharaoh's guard. In spite of his having been badly spoiled, there is good in Joseph and adversity brings the good in him to the surface. From having been the favorite son of a rich man, he is now a slave in a foreign land. But he serves well and is soon appointed overseer for his master. Bad luck isn't over, though. The master's wife, a wealthy woman without enough to occupy her, thinks that an affair with this handsome young Hebrew would be fun. Joseph, however, refuses. She is furious at his rejection and accuses him of rape. He is imprisoned.

The fact that Joseph was not put to death says something about how impressed his master must have been with him. Perhaps he also knew his wife pretty well. Anyway, in prison Joseph again does so well that he becomes an overseer there. Obviously he is a born leader. The butler and the baker of the pharaoh's court are also imprisoned, and each has a dream that he cannot interpret. Joseph reveals the meanings of the dreams, one good and one bad. The baker is put to death as Joseph had prophesied; the butler is restored to his place, where he promptly forgets a promise made to Joseph that he would intercede for him.

Two long years go by and the ruler of Egypt has a dream that none of his seers can explain. (It is hard for us today to realize how important dreams were held to be in Bible times, but they were.) The butler says, in effect, "Oh dear! I forgot all about that nice young man in jail," and tells the pharaoh about Joseph being able to interpret dreams. Joseph is sent for, and after he is made presentable, he is brought before the pharaoh and interprets the pharaoh's dream. You may remember the pharaoh's dream about the seven fat cattle devoured by the lean and likewise the seven full ears of corn, and of Joseph's prophecy of the seven good years to be followed by seven of famine. So there is another rapid change in Joseph's fortunes. At the age of thirty, he becomes Egypt's comptroller—not to mention secretary of agriculture! In the ensuing seven years, he has an excellent conservation and storage program, so when the famine strikes on schedule, Egypt is the one area that does not suffer and has enough grain to sell to foreigners.

In the dramatic denouement, we find that, with Canaan in the grip of famine, Jacob has no choice but to send his sons to Egypt to buy food. The story of Joseph's encounters with his brothers makes fascinating reading. Joseph can't refrain from testing them—and indeed who could blame him? He waits for the right moment, and while waiting he finds that by living with their father's grief they have indeed changed. They are now willing to sacrifice themselves to spare Jacob the loss of Benjamin. Finally there is a joyful reunion, and all of Jacob's household, his flocks, and herds—all Abraham's descendants—end up in Egypt in the land of Goshen, apparently prime pasturage, as honored guests of Egypt's ruler. Impressive evidence of Joseph's wisdom and forgiving spirit come through when he tells his brothers not to blame themselves any longer for their sin against him (Gen. 45:5).

The book of Genesis ends with the death of Joseph some seven decades later. He is embalmed in the Egyptian manner for eventual burial in Canaan.

4

The Exodus

Exodus

The action in the book of Exodus begins about three hundred years after the close of Genesis. During those three centuries, the number of Jews has greatly increased, different pharaohs have ascended the throne, and the position of the Hebrews has changed from esteemed guests to slaves. This may have happened under Rameses II, known as "The Builder," who used a great deal of slave labor.

There is considerable difficulty as to the exact dates for the Exodus and the conquest of Canaan. Anywhere from 1290 to 1220 B.C.E. has support. At any rate, the ruling monarch in the opening chapter of Exodus not only wants more work from the slaves, but is afraid that in a war (one usually being in the offing), a rebellion of the slaves might well tip the scales in favor of the enemy. So he orders that all male children born to the Hebrews be drowned. Again we find a very familiar story: the child Moses hidden by his mother as long as possible and then placed in a basket of rushes.

In the King James Version this basket is called an ark (see Ex. 2:3)—the second time an ark has been involved in deliverance. The pharaoh's daughter finds the baby and coincidently the baby's own mother is hired to care for him. He grows up with an impressive background: the culture and sophistication of the ruling class of an ancient civilization. Yet with all his Hebrew heritage, which was evidently drilled into him by his mother, the Scriptures tell us that when he is grown he sees an Egyptian overseer mistreating a Jewish slave and kills the official. He then flees into the Midian Desert and remains there for some time, marrying the daughter of Jethro, a priest. While keeping his father-in-law's sheep on Mount Horeb (Sinai? We don't know for sure), Moses has an encounter with God, and the course of history is changed.

It is in Exodus that the Hebrew concept of God begins to come clear and solidifies into the stubbornly monotheistic view of a Jehovah, a God who acts in human affairs and who is infinitely above the hodgepodge of mythological and nature cults current in the other nations of the ancient world. This God tells Moses that his destiny is to lead the Hebrews out of slavery and back into the Promised Land. Instead of being eager and flattered, Moses is about as reluctant an instrument of God's will as can be imagined. He says, in effect, "Who, me?" His excuses range from a fear that neither the Jews nor Pharaoh will listen to him to the fact that he's no public speaker. (Does that sound familiar?) But God finally overrides Moses' objections, and when he is finally convinced of this he does indeed make a steadfast and intrepid leader. He is an outstanding example of what God can do with a less than enthusiastic tool.

You will no doubt remember the means used to force Pharaoh to release the Jews: ten plagues, the water turned to blood, frogs, lice, flies, murrain of cattle, boils, hail, locusts, darkness, and finally the death of the firstborn of the Egyptians. There have been, of course, attempts to explain these by natural means: that Goshen was probably the healthiest section of Egypt, or perhaps because the Hebrews were toughened by hard labor and spartan diets, they were better fitted to withstand disease. Again I cannot feel that it really matters whether God used natural or supernatural means. At any rate, Pharaoh finally let them go, and there is the institution of the Passover, still perhaps the most important of the high holy days to the Jewish people.

The whole idea of the mechanics of the Exodus staggers the mind. I am inclined to cast a somewhat jaundiced eye on the biblical pictures done by Hollywood. But certainly in the production *The Ten Commandments* one gets a magnificent picture of what was involved: the noise, the confusion, the desperate haste, and the feeling of awe for what Jehovah has done.

One problem that recurs in the Bible might as well be dealt with here—the exaggeration of numbers. The Bible is fairly casual about several things. Certainly time is one of them. For example, only very careful New Testament reading will disclose the fact that some thirteen years passed between Paul's conversion and his acceptance by the apostles. Actually we are warned about this by the psalmist when we are reminded that a thousand years are but a day in the sight of God. But the concept of large numbers is also tricky. Have you never said, "I have about a thousand things I need to do today"? which, being translated, probably comes up to five or six. It appears inescapable that the six hundred thousand men, plus women and children, mentioned in Exodus 12:37 must be taken as this kind of hyperbole. If the Hebrews in Egypt had numbered around two million, there would have been no need for them to be slaves. The land of Goshen could have supported only a few thousand and likewise with the Sinai Peninsula.

William Neil thinks that five thousand is a reasonable estimate of the people led out by Moses[1], and I see no reason to quarrel with this. Certainly five thousand stiff-necked Hebrews were quite enough to cope with! Most scholars put Rameses's army at around twenty thousand. If considering the record as literary exaggeration bothers you, there are other possibilities: a mistake in translation, a misplaced census from the time of David, when two-and-a-half million Jews would be an acceptable count, that the word *thousand* can sometimes be translated as *clan;* or the writer can be implying that all of Israel, including Jews from a much later date, was redeemed in the Exodus—the same sort of reasoning that inspired the spiritual, "Were you there when they crucified my Lord?"

Anyway, in their flight they come to a body of water (known most commonly as the Red Sea) with the Egyptian chariots pursuing. Exactly what this water was, we do not know. The "Red Sea" translation is inaccurate. The oldest manuscripts have "Sea of Reeds," implying a marshy area. Various possibilities have been put forward: what is now the Gulf of Suez, the Gulf of Aqabah, or another arm of the Red Sea, or an inland freshwater lake. Again I cannot see that it really matters. A body of water blocks their way. By God's hand (using a strong east wind), they are able to get across. The winds and currents in that area are erratic, and it is sometimes possible to see the sand below the water in many places. Whether the crossing involved a natural phenomenon or not, the timing would surely constitute a miracle. Their pursuers are caught by the returning waters. With iron chariots there would be no chance of escape,

---

[1]See *Harper's Bible Commentary,* by William Neil. Copyright © 1962 by Hodder & Stoughton Ltd. New York: Harper & Row, 1962, p. 79. Used by permission.

especially if there were quicksand in spots. So the people are free, and Moses and Miriam lead them in triumphant song.

Yet forty years go by before they reach the Promised Land—forty years during which the people alternately praise and curse God and Moses, worship devoutly, and then fall into sin. God blesses them. They respond. Then, they fall away, are punished, repent, and are given another chance. The cycle repeats all over again. How often do we see the same sort of thing in our own lives—fluctuations of faith and of doubt, of worship and of rebellion?

Included in the book of Exodus is, of course, the story of the Ten Commandments. Just before this there is a third covenant at Sinai: "Now, therefore if ye will obey my voice indeed, and keep my covenant, then ye shall be a peculiar treasure unto me above all people: for all the earth *is* mine" (Ex. 19:5). Then the commandments are given. Moses is gone a long time, and meanwhile, back at the ranch (or rather back at the foot of the mountain), the people become impatient and talk Aaron, Moses' brother and spokesman, into making an idol—the golden calf. Both Yahweh and Moses are incensed. Moses breaks the tablets, and the ringleaders of the revolt are put to death. Moses intercedes for the people and the commandments are given a second time.

Also in Exodus, we find instructions for the making of the tabernacle and the ark (which would signify the presence of Jehovah in their midst), and the presence above it of a pillar of cloud by day and a pillar of fire by night, among other stories. The close of Exodus comes when the people have been gone from Egypt a little more than a year.

Leviticus

The book of Leviticus gets its name from Levi, the priestly tribe. It can be called the laws of the Levites or the "Priestly Manual," though these laws are not confined to this book (there is a lot of law in both Exodus and Numbers). Detailed instructions for worship and sacrifice and laws concerning food, discipline, and punishment for various offenses are found in this book of the Bible. Remember that at this time the Hebrews had no civil or criminal code, no pure food and drug act; this was it. There are some amazingly modern and practical ideas, such as crop rotation, capital punishment, no discrimination against foreigners.

Certainly Leviticus is one of the harder books in the Bible as far as interesting reading goes. Some of it makes for reading that is fascinating, horrifying, and even boring. There is very little narrative in it and endless details. But a scanning of it will bring certain rewards in a perspective on what the life of the people of that time was like. Many of its instructions are very old, but it was probably not put into its present form until long after the Exodus, possibly as late as seven hundred B.C.E. One thing it does is to make clear that there was a moral basis for almost every part of the ritual.

Numbers

The book of Numbers gets its name from a census taken of the tribes to establish a count of men fit to fight. This is done by the twelve tribes, with the priests being exempt from war by reason of their priestly function even as ministers and theological students have not been subject to the draft in our own time. The same problem with figures arises here in Numbers as it did at the beginning of the Exodus. Yet along with the arithmetic, there is a good deal of narrative in Numbers, along with more law. The desert wanderings continue, and at one point the tribes draw near to Canaan. Spies are sent to look things over, one from each tribe (for more detail read ch. 13). All twelve report on the goodness of the land and its desirability, but ten say that it is impossible to conquer. Only two, Caleb from the tribe of Joshua and Joshua from Ephraim, say that with the Lord's help they can overcome the inhabitants. After hearing the reports, the people are bitterly discouraged and say that they would be better off dead (Num. 14:2) and are ready to elect a captain to lead them back to Egypt to slavery—and security. How often are we ready to put security ahead of any venture toward daring in the *doing* of God's will?

Once again God is ready to write off all the people except for Moses and to fulfill his purpose through Moses' line alone. But again Moses intercedes for his flock, and once again God listens and holds his hand. But this time there is a condition—and a hard one. None of those who left Egypt as adults will live to enter Canaan, with the exception of Caleb and Joshua, the two spies who had sufficient faith to vote for the invasion. This, of course, is where the forty years comes in.

In the rest of Numbers, the division of the land is spelled out, Aaron dies, there is war with some of the neighboring tribes (notably the Midianites), and Numbers ends with the tribes encamped on the plains of Moab across from Jericho. In 1 Corinthians, Paul sees the years in the wilderness as a time of testing for the people, as indeed it was. But there was more. It was a time of unification for the diverse peoples who had come out of Egypt. It was also a time for shaping an army that would be able to conquer the land. It behooves us today to remember that the same sins that beset the people and are spelled out in Numbers still plague us today: greed, discontent, lack of faith, lust, and cowardice.

Deuteronomy

When we come to Deuteronomy we find that most of it is repetition; the name itself means "second law." In it is Moses' farewell speech to the Israelites where he reminds them of all that God has done in their behalf and of how often they have been rebellious and disobedient. He exhorts them to worship and obey Jehovah, and he repeats many of the laws spelled out earlier. The heart of Moses' message is found in chapters 30 and 31:

"I command thee this day to love the LORD thy God, to walk in his ways, and to keep his commandments . . . that thou mayest live and multiply: and the LORD thy God shall bless thee in the land whither thou goest to possess it" (Deut. 30:16).

"Be strong and of a good courage, fear not . . . for the LORD thy God . . . doth go with thee; he will not fail thee, nor forsake thee" (Deut. 31:6).

At the close of the book Moses dies. He has seen the Promised Land, but does not enter into it. His task is finished.

5

The Promised Land

Joshua

With the book of Joshua (named for Moses' successor as leader and general), we find the people, after a month of mourning for Moses, ready to go into Canaan. What was this land that they had dreamed of and looked forward to for nearly a half century?

In size, Canaan was very small—less than 150 miles long and on an average about forty miles wide, the approximate size of Belgium. The climate and terrain have great variation. Mount Hermon is about 9100 feet above sea level while the Dead Sea is 1290 feet below sea level. Jerusalem has a moderate climate with an altitude of 2600 feet; however, only fifteen miles away at Jericho, it is tropical and 825 feet below sea level. Roughly speaking, the Promised Land for the Hebrews comprised most of what is today Israel, Jordan, Syria, and Lebanon. This area is relatively small, but certainly one of the most important spots in the world, religiously and historically.

Into this small but infinitely exciting land go the Hebrews, and in the books of Joshua and Judges we have the accounts of the conquest—and a bloody business it is. There is a savagery and a ruthlessness in these books that we find almost impossible to accept in the light of Christ's teachings. Blood, sweat, and tears are in abundance. We must remember, however, that these were hard and rugged times, and it was commonplace for people to fight for the possession of land. For that matter, is it so different today? We have only to look at the struggles over land in that same territory in our time or to remember when the Europeans took the land from the native Americans not so long ago.

Early in Joshua we get the story of Rahab the harlot, who befriended the two spies sent into Jericho by Joshua; the people crossing over the Jordan; and the fall of Jericho after seven days of circling the city with a continuous noise of trumpets. I used to think this worked on the same principle as shattering a glass with a violin note. I also recall that when we lived near New York, the belief was current that if all the cars in the Holland Tunnel were to blow their horns at a given instant, the tunnel would collapse. At any rate, Jericho was subdued, and many other victories, along with some defeats, followed. However, details of these and the careful description of just how the land is apportioned are not important in an overall look of this kind. The covenant is renewed at Shechem: "Now therefore fear the LORD, and serve him in sincerity and in truth" (Josh. 24:14). And, the people said unto Joshua, "The LORD our God will we serve, and his voice will we obey. So Joshua made a covenant with the people that day" (Josh. 24:24-25).

It is worth remembering, in reading both Joshua and Judges, that the Bible isn't much interested in politics, economics, or warfare for their own sakes. It is, instead, what they tell us about the hand of God at work. History and prophecy are wonderfully intermingled in the narrative books of the Bible and reflect the conviction of its writers that God was indeed acting in history for his own purposes.

Judges

Judges continues the account of conquest and settlement and gives a picture of the life of the people between their first arrival and the establishment of the kingdom some one hundred and fifty years later. The conquest of Canaan under Joshua can be put at around 1250 B.C.E., with the beginning of the monarchy at approximately 1000 B.C.E. The actual rule of the judges comes out at between 150 and 200 years, give or take a few. This was a chaotic and hectic period. Parts of the land were conquered and at peace and ruled by local leaders called judges. Other parts were still fighting, with their leaders more military men than politicians. There are fascinating, shocking, and repelling stories in the book, such as Ehud, the left-handed slayer of the king of Moab. There's also the well-known story of Samson and Delilah, that timeless source of drama and opera with its hero so flawed by his own appetites. Samson is so naive in his dealing with women that he is a perfect illustration of the Bible's refusal to soften the picture of its mighty men. Then there's Deborah, a prophetess, judge, and warrior; Gideon and his classic example of military strategy as opposed to numbers, and many, many more. Toward the end of the book, a good deal of fighting among the various tribes is reported.

It is important to realize that there were many different situations in different parts of the country. In some areas the Hebrews simply settled down with the former inhabitants fairly peaceably and considerable intermarriage occurred. In other places, the inhabitants were either all killed or completely driven out to wander. In still others, they were made slaves. There was, in short, no unity worthy of the name. Judges closes with an apt verse: "In those days *there was* no king in Israel: every man did *that which was* right in his own eyes" (Judg. 21:25). Turbulence in Canaan was the order of the day, compounded by the entry of the Hebrews from the east and the Philistines from the southeast. Yet in the midst of this chaos, the Hebrews felt that God was working to weld a new unity and to deliver the land into their hands.

Ruth

Next comes the beautiful little book of Ruth, and what a contrast to the blood and thunder of Joshua and Judges! The incidents recorded here took place during the period of the Judges, and remind us that while fighting and jockeying for position were going on, the common people were still planting and harvesting crops, marrying and giving birth. In short, life went on.

The book of Ruth tells of a family in Judah, who had been forced by famine, an ancient scourge and unfortunately a modern one as well, to go and live in Moab, a foreign land across the Jordan River. The father and two sons died there, and the mother, Naomi, is left with her two daughters-in-law, both of Moab. She decides to return to her home in Bethlehem, not expecting her daughters-in-law to go with her. One doesn't. But Ruth refuses to desert her mother-in-law in some of the most beautiful words ever written: "whither thou goest, I will go . . . thy people *shall be* my people, and thy God my God" (Ruth 1:16). In Bethlehem, Ruth gleans after the harvesters to support herself and Naomi. With a little judicious matchmaking on Naomi's part, Ruth and Boaz (a family connection of Naomi's) are married, and there is a happy ending.

Why is this lovely little story in the Bible? Just as a relief from battles and bloodshed? By no means. Ruth and Boaz have a son, Obed, whose son is Jesse, the father of David. In other words, the great-grandmother was a Gentile; and the blood of a foreigner ran in David's veins. Remember back in Genesis when God told Abraham that all humanity was to be blessed through him—not just the Jews? In Ruth, God is saying again that there is room in his love for all people—that Moabites and other outsiders can also be his chosen.

First and Second Samuel

When we get to 1 and 2 Samuel (originally one book), we find the Israelites a more settled people: planting crops, living in towns as well as tents, and with a fairly complete fusion between the Hebrews and the Canaanites who remained after the conquest. We also find that a good deal of the Canaanite religion (notably the worship of Baal) has crept into the faith of the Hebrews. It is this that concerns Samuel, Nathan, and Elijah most.

First Samuel opens with the birth of Samuel and his dedication to the Lord. He spends his time with the priest, Eli, in the holy house at Shiloh. When he is grown, he becomes not only prophet and priest but the last and greatest of the judges. There is still fighting at this time, mainly with the Philistines. Through Samuel's intercession and the people's promise to put away strange gods and to serve the Lord, they are given a decisive victory. When Samuel grows old, he, like Eli before him, is disappointed in his sons, who are not fit to succeed him. At this time the people demand a king to rule over them: "That we also may be like all the nations" (1 Sam. 8:20). How many mistakes have been made in order to be like everybody else! Samuel tells them that they will rue the day they asked for a king—that taxes will be high and that there will be forced labor. But they refuse to listen. So the Lord tells Samuel to go along with their request, and he anoints Saul of the tribe of Benjamin.

Saul starts out well, but in another war against the Philistines he is arrogant and disobedient. After a reign of about two years, God no longer favors Saul; and David, of the tribe of Judah, is secretly anointed by Samuel. David becomes armor bearer to Saul and a close friend of Saul's son, Jonathan. Eventually we get the famous conflict between

David and Goliath, the great warrior of the Philistine host, in which David is victorious with a slingshot and a stone. At first this makes him Saul's favorite, but Saul's love turns to jealousy because of the people's adulation for David. The Scripture reads "And the women . . . said, Saul hath slain his thousands, and David his ten thousands. And Saul was very wroth, and the saying displeased him" (1 Sam. 18:7-8). Apparently this triggers a lasting enmity on Saul's part, and although David becomes his son-in-law, Saul continues to plot against him.

A good deal of the material through here, like that in Joshua and Judges, is difficult for us. The idea of a holy war, where all of the enemy, their children, and even their possessions must be destroyed, goes against the grain. However, we have to remember that Christ has not yet come—that the New Testament concept of love, so dear to us, was as yet unknown. But what about after Christ had come? How much has really changed? How many crimes have been committed in the name of Christianity? What about the Crusades? the Spanish Inquisition? How many bloody wars have been fought with each party convinced that God was on their side? In the First World War the rallying cry of the Germans was "Gott mitt us."[1] We shudder at the idea of total destruction, but what about Vietnam and the use of napalm? And as far as a religious war goes, at least in name, we have only to look at the state of the Ireland of our day and other countries around the world. None of this completely reconciles me to the violence in the Old Testament, but it is there, and there is no use ignoring it.

Saul made numerous attempts to rid himself of David, whom increasingly he sees as a deadly rival. David's life is saved once by his wife, Michal, and a couple of times his life is saved by Jonathan. On several occasions David has a chance to kill Saul, but holds his hand, still hoping that their differences can be resolved. David's character in these early years comes through as generous, open, warmhearted, and devout. Indeed, as the Bible tells us, David is a man after God's own heart. Saul is a complex and fascinating person—his own worst enemy. Scholars have speculated that he was plagued by migraine, because we read that he often had spells of some sort. Early in their relationship, David would play his harp to soothe the ailing monarch.

---

[1]Translation: God with us.

Undoubtedly Saul was neurotic, and by the end very possibly psychotic.

Finally, in a losing battle with the Philistines, Jonathan is killed and Saul commits suicide. David mourns them both. This comes at the end of 1 Samuel, and not far into 2 Samuel we read, "How are the mighty fallen, And the weapons of war perished!" (2 Sam. 1:27).

Second Samuel

David is made king over Judah (the southern part of the country), but war continues between him and the house of Saul. Somewhere along the line, David has acquired several more wives, who are busily bearing sons (and presumably daughters, but they don't count for much, except for when they get into trouble and must be avenged by their brothers). David becomes increasingly powerful, victorious in battle, tremendously wealthy, and very popular with the common people. He is made king over Israel (the northern section) as well as Judah. He establishes the capital of this united kingdom at Jerusalem, wrenching it from the Jebusites in a military coup by sending men up a water shaft. From here on, Jerusalem is the Holy City, the City of David, and of tremendous importance in the religious life of the Jewish people. In Jerusalem, the ark of the tabernacle is installed still in a tent. David builds a palace for himself, but is told by God that the building of God's temple is to be left for David's son, Solomon. David's prosperity continues and increases, the kingdom finally stretches from the Gulf of Aqabah in the south to beyond Damascus in the north, and from the Mediterranean Sea on across the Jordan River into the desert to the east. It is a well-organized monarchy, with delegated authority to the military, the priesthood, and the secular powers. Along with his battles and his setting up of the details of his rule, David takes time out to seek for remaining members of the house of Saul—not in vengeance, but in compassion. He finds that a lame son of Jonathan has survived and is living in poverty. David brings him into the palace and treats him as a son.

Around 1000 B.C.E. David becomes king in Jerusalem, and he rules approximately thirty years. Rich, powerful, and popular, he established a commonwealth that is regarded by later Jews as the pinnacle of their history, a golden age indeed. It was this sort of a kingdom that most of Christ's disciples a millennium later wanted him to bring about. This hope explains in some degree why they were so dense about what Christ's kingdom was really to be.

So it seems as though David has, within his possession, all that a mortal man could desire. Someone said, and for the life of me I can't remember who it was—"Power corrupts. Absolute power corrupts absolutely." David was a despot, and his power was very close to being absolute. One evening from the roof of his palace he looked down upon another roof and saw a very beautiful woman bathing. On inquiring, he discovers that her name is Bathsheba, and that she is the wife of one of his generals. This does not deter him. He wants her, sends for her, and goes to bed with her. No matter that by this time David has a great many wives as well as a number of concubines. What he saw and wanted, he took. We do not know Bathsheba's feelings, whether she was flattered, frightened, willing, or unwilling. The only words we have from her are recorded in 2 Samuel 11:5 in the message she sent to David when she discovers she is pregnant:"I *am* with child."

Now while it was perfectly acceptable for a monarch in that time and place to have many wives and concubines, it was not acceptable for him to commit adultery with the wife of one of his loyal soldiers. In an attempt to avoid disaster, David sends for Uriah, presumably to report on the war, hoping that he will lie with his wife while at home and that the child can then be passed off as Uriah's. It was not the first time, nor the last, for this kind of ploy. A good many families somewhere in their history can find a "premature" eight-pound baby! Uriah, however, is too conscientious a man to fall in with David's plan. Since the soldiers under him have been without their wives for many months, Uriah will share their abstinence. In desperation David then sends Uriah back to the front with a letter to the commanding general, Joab, that Uriah is to be placed in the forefront of the hottest battle and that Joab is then to withdraw the supporting troops so that Uriah is sure to be killed. It is a measure of David's panic that he would thus put himself in the hands of Joab! The thing is done, Uriah's death is duly announced to David and to Bathsheba. The record says simply that "she mourned for her husband" (2 Sam. 11:26). With its remarkable economy of words, the Bible tells us nothing more of her feelings. After the mourning period is over she becomes David's wife, and in due time bears a son. Second Samuel 11 ends with the spare statement, "But the thing that David had done displeased the LORD."

In the next chapter David is confronted by the prophet Nathan, who tells him a moving tale of a rich man with many sheep and a poor man with one pet lamb. The rich man, to entertain a guest, takes the poor man's lamb to be slaughtered instead of one of his own. David's generous heart is touched, and he cries out that the rich man should surely be put to death. In an exceedingly dramatic moment, Nathan simply says to him, "Thou art the man." And instead of putting the prophet to death, a probable reaction from most potentates of the time, David listens while Nathan details his sin and pronounces the punishment: that the sword will never depart from David's house. David confesses that he has indeed, "sinned against the LORD" (2 Sam. 12:13)—not to mention against Uriah.

Psalm 51, long attributed to David's repentance after Nathan's confrontation, is a beautiful, abject, and humble expression of penitence. David is forgiven and his relationship with God restored. This does not, however, remove the consequences of sin. The child begotten in adultery dies, and though another son, Solomon, is born of Bathsheba, family troubles of one sort or another plague David for the rest of his days. It is worth remembering that while God's forgiveness is always ours for the asking, this does not necessarily mean blue skies again. Sin, unrepented or confessed and forgiven, still carries consequences. In David's case, the climax of his trouble comes when a favorite son, Absalom, plots a revolt against his father, and in the putting down of the rebellion Absalom is killed. David's grief is great "O my son Absalom! my son, my son Absalom! would God I had died for thee, O Absalom, my son, my son!" (2 Sam. 18:33).

David surely is one of the most fascinating of the Old Testament characters. Many authors have written novels around his life. In all books, plays, and movies based on biblical material, the one thing to watch is what you know is actually in the Bible and what is the product of the author's imagination. With this in mind, a good deal of biblical fiction can prove valuable in bringing a period alive, or fleshing out the bare bones of a character.

An interesting incident closes 2 Samuel. A fierce pestilence attacks the people, and David wants an altar and animals for sacrifice in a hope that the plague may be lifted. He tries to buy the threshing floor of one of his subjects, Araunah. But Araunah wants to give both it and the animals to David, for David is his king. David's words "neither will I offer . . . unto the LORD my God of that which doth cost me nothing" (2 Sam. 24:24) have made an excellent text for many stewardship sermons.

First and Second Kings

Early in 1 Kings, David, under some pressure from Bathsheba, names Solomon as his heir, and exhorts him to be faithful to the Lord. David dies and is buried in Jerusalem. Solomon starts out extremely well, asking God for wisdom to rule wisely. Wisdom is granted, and the early and dramatic example of it is given in the story of his decision concerning the two women and their infants, one of which has been smothered in the night, and both mothers claiming the living child. You remember that Solomon, depending on the love of the real mother to make her willing to surrender the baby, decrees that the child be cut in half, one part for each. Of course, by this means he determines who the child's mother is (1 Kings 3:16–28).

Solomon was not only a wise man. He was a great builder, erecting the great Temple at Jerusalem, which was the very lifeblood of later generations of Jewish people. He was a patron of literature and a commercial genius. He had a fleet of merchant ships and developed copper and iron mines. He was even a horse trader, and in recent years, some of his magnificent stables have been excavated, rivalling some of the racing establishments of our day around Lexington, Kentucky. Under him the kingdom was rich and powerful and culture flourished. You will remember that the Queen of Sheba, no mean monarch in her own right, was greatly impressed.

But Solomon had many faults, and, like his father before him, too much power was a part of his downfall. For his building and his armies, he conscripted labor; Hebrew men had to serve one month out of three, and being forced into such a system was extremely grievous to proud Jews, reminding them of their forbears' slavery in Egypt. Taxes, too, became increasingly burdensome to support Solomon and his court in the expensive luxury he had grown to love. And his final and most important mistake was, quite simply, too many women. He married many times, often for some political advantage, and he had an extensive harem of concubines as well. The majority of his women were of religions other than the worship of Jehovah, and apparently Solomon became intellectually intrigued by these various cults and rituals, to the point where "his wives turned away his heart after other gods . . . .And Solomon did evil in the sight of the LORD" (1 Kings 11:4, 6).After a forty-year reign Solomon died and things fell apart.

Saul, David, and Solomon have all been written off as failures. Their pursuit of power politics, of wealth and self-indulgence, along with their inability to keep the people true to Jehovah, have found them wanting in the eyes of God. From Solomon's death on, deterioration was rapid. He was succeeded by his son, Rehoboam, who had all of his father's arrogance and none of his early wisdom. When the people asked him for relief from the heavy taxes, his answer was to increase them. The northern ten tribes revolted, and Jeroboam, a former overseer of Solomon's, became their king. From here on for about two centuries the kingdom was divided: the Northern Kingdom, which was Galilee, Samaria, and environs, with ten of the tribes as inhabitants (now known as Israel), and the Southern Kingdom—Judea with the two tribes of Judah and Benjamin and eastward (the kingdom of Judah).

The record of the two centuries following Solomon's death is for the most part a sorry tale. In Israel, during this period, there are nineteen rulers—all of them bad.We read over and over that the king did what was evil in the sight of the Lord, and that the people did not walk in the way of the Lord.

The worst ruler of all was Ahab, and yet he was not as bad as his wife, Jezebel, who did her best to turn all of Israel to the worship of Baal.We get during these years the stories of the prophet Elijah, with the most dramatic story being his contest with the prophets of Baal. The story goes that on Mount Carmel there is an altar with a fire laid for sacrifice.All day, Baal's prophets call on him to light the fire, with no success and with some fairly funny jeers from Elijah (1 Kings 18:27).Then, with the instincts of a good showman, Elijah has water poured all over the wood and the altar before calling upon Jehovah, who, in a tremendous scene of vindication for Elijah's faith, sends a consuming fire that even licks up the water. The people fall to their knees and cry, "The LORD, he *is* the God" (1 Kings 18:39).And at the same time the long drought is broken and there is a "sound of abundance of rain" (1 Kings 18:41).

Many fascinating stories are recorded in 1 and 2 Kings: wars between Israel and Judah, but also alliances between them; war between Israel and Syria; tales of Jehu and his chariot, of Naaman the leper of Syria and his healing by Elisha, the prophet who succeeded Elijah; of famine in Samaria; of murder and intrigue. There are times when things look brighter and Israel is prosperous. But it doesn't last. Finally, in 721 B.C.E, Israel is overrun and conquered by Assyria. This is the last we hear in the Bible of those northern ten tribes. They are scattered. Some carried away. From here on, the story of the chosen people goes through the Southern Kingdom of Judah.

Back in the Southern Kingdom things have gone a little better, though not much. After Solomon's death, around 922 B.C.E., Judah has, in the next three-and-a-half centuries, twenty kings and one queen. Most of them are bad, but there are notable exceptions. One was Joash, who came to the throne at the age of seven. In a long reign (forty years) "he did that which was right in the sight of the Lord" (2 Kings 14:3). He also bribed the king of Syria, so that Jerusalem was saved. Hezekiah was another good king, with twenty-nine years on the throne. It was while he was ruler that Sennacherib of Assyria besieged Jerusalem, and that, by striking the Assyrian camp with a plague, God delivered the city. It is this incident that is celebrated in Byron's poem, beginning, "The Assyrian came down like a wolf on the fold ... "[2]

Josiah was the last of the good kings, with a thirty-one-year reign. Though he restored the Temple and the reading of the law and sought with all his might to turn the people back to God, he could not halt the rush to disaster by men and women who refused to see that power, wealth, prestige, and a false sense of security that these fostered were not what life was all about for the children of Jehovah. The prophets had tried to tell both Israel and Judah that they were headed for disaster but to no avail (we will look more closely at this when we get to the prophetic books). It is easy to condemn Israel and Judah, and much harder to take an unprejudiced look at ourselves. By

---

[2]From "The Destruction of Sennacherib," in "Hebrew Melodies," by Lord Byron, found in *Bartlett's Familiar Quotations*. Fifteenth Edition. Copyright © 1955, 1965, 1968, 1980 by Little, Brown and Company. Boston: Little, Brown and Company, 1980, p. 459.

and large, we can be pretty selfish, arrogant, and greedy people too—the almighty dollar has its effect on most of us.

So, in 587 B.C.E., about a century-and-a-half after the fall of Israel, Judah also goes down in defeat at the hands of Babylon. Jerusalem is laid waste by Nebuchadnezzar. The Temple is sacked, and the able-bodied among the people are carried away into captivity. It looks as if the promises made to Abraham and to Moses have been canceled out. The land of milk and honey now flows with blood and tears as we come to the end of 2 Kings.

1 and 2 Chronicles

The books of 1 and 2 Chronicles, also originally one book, are almost in their entirety a retelling of events found in the books of Samuel and of Kings. They were written later (well after the exile and the return to Jerusalem), and from a different point of view. In a brief study such as this, we will spend no time on them.

Ezra and Nehemiah

The exile lasts for fifty years, or about a generation. But strangely enough, there is very little in the Bible about that half century. It seems as if there should be a book between the close of Kings and the opening of Ezra. Perhaps someday, another manuscript will be discovered, for those fifty years were tremendously important! We learn a fair amount about them from some of the prophetic books written during that time. For example, we are given glimpses from parts of Jeremiah and all of Lamentations, and some from the Psalms—notably the 137th: "By the rivers of Babylon, . . . we wept, When we remembered Zion. . . . How shall we sing the LORD's song In a strange land?" (vs. 1, 4).

Certainly those were years of suffering and bitterness. They had thought that the Holy City was indestructible, that the house of David could never be completely overthrown. They found that they were wrong. Yet what happened to the people during the captivity was, next to the Exodus, the most important period in Old Testament history. They learned as captives that God meant more to them in trouble than in prosperity. When do you pray most earnestly? When all is going well or when your world falls apart? They learned also that they could worship in a small group in the synagogue as well or better than in the great Temple. They truly began once more to see themselves as a people set apart, ruled by the laws given to Moses. The prophets, notably Ezekiel, Isaiah, and Hosea, tell the people that God has not forgotten them—that a remnant (a very important word in prophecy) is to have another chance.

And that comes about through another conqueror, Cyrus of Persia. He overcomes Babylon, as Babylon had earlier conquered Assyria, and makes himself master of the largest area any one person had ruled up to that time. This happened in 538 B.C.E. Cyrus's enlightened policy was to permit his subjects to live in their homelands, and, consequently, he permitted all the Jews who wished to do so to return to Jerusalem. Many do, during the years 539–520 B.C.E., though undoubtedly another trickle came with Ezra and a few more with Nehemiah. Under Ezra, a priest, and Nehemiah, a governor, the wall around the city is rebuilt, the Temple is repaired, and a community of law is established.

The timing on all this is a little tricky, partly because the chronicler of these events did not specify whether he meant Darius I or II and ditto with Xerxes and Artaxerxes (there were two of each). Many scholars think that the books should be reversed—that Nehemiah came back some time before Ezra did. At any rate, under harassment by enemies (notably the Samaritans) and against great odds (but encouraged by the prophets Haggai and Zechariah as well as by Ezra and Nehemiah), the task was accomplished: "So built we the wall; . . . for the people had a mind to work . . . . *every one* with one of his hands wrought in the work, and with the other *hand* held a weapon" (Neh. 4:6, 17). Ezra and his supporters, and, to a somewhat lesser degree, Nehemiah and his, were firmly convinced that the captivity had been punishment from Yahweh because the people had turned away from him. Now that a remnant had a second chance, their leaders were determined that they weren't going to blow it a second time.

With this certainly laudable aim, they believed a precious legacy of the covenant relationship with God was to be handed on. Unfortunately, the way they went about it was to concentrate on ritual and minute observance of the Mosaic law rather than on justice and love of God. They developed a law so rigid and a racism so exclusive (to keep from being contaminated by lesser faiths) that the Jewish nation becomes a byword for intolerance—a people to be shunned by other nations. It remained for Christ, some four hundred years later, to teach that love was greater than law.

With the close of Nehemiah, we come to the end of the chronological story of the Old Testament. The books that follow run concurrently with events that have already taken place. Now, of course, the dates of the writing of the books are quite different from the times of the events recorded. The latest book written in the Old Testament was in all probability Daniel—at least the latter part, which can be placed at about 167 B.C.E. But the actual story, from Abraham to the return of the exiles and the rebuilding of Jerusalem, covers around sixteen hundred years. In contrast, the New Testament story covers less than seventy years.

Esther

The next book in the sequence in our Bible is Esther, a rousing good story that takes place just following the captivity in the Persian Empire probably during the time covered in Ezra and Nehemiah. The book had a hard time getting into the canon, mainly because God's name is not mentioned. It has all the elements of a romance-suspense tale: a beauty contest, a lovely heroine in deadly danger but with rare courage, and certainly a wicked villain. You probably remember the story: Ahasuerus (Artaxerxes), king of Persia, gives a stag party and decides he wants his number one wife, Vashti, to display her beauty for his guests. She refuses (showing quite as much courage as Esther does later), and this causes a real flap. All the male guests agree that if the queen gets away with this it will surely undermine their domestic authority. She is deposed and a replacement sought.

Among the Hebrew captives in the Persian court are Mordecai and his young cousin, Esther, who wins the contest and succeeds Vashti. Haman, the villain, plots against Mordecai and all the Jews in the area, and gets the king to sign a decree that on a certain date all shall be put to death. (If this sounds arbitrary and fantastic, just think back to Hitler and the death of six million Jews.) Mordecai tells Esther she must intercede with the king—a very risky thing to do. But she does it, after Mordecai's words, "[W]ho knoweth whether thou art come to the kingdom for *such* a time as this?" (Esth. 4:14), and there is a happy though bloody ending, with the villain put to death. We get the expression "hanged as high as Haman" from this book.

The Jewish Feast of Purim is a celebration of the book of Esther. Luther had a comment about the book which tickles me. He said it was too full of "heathen naughtiness." I have always wondered how he rationalized some of the nonheathen naughtiness recorded in Scripture.

6

The Wisdom Literature

Job

The next five books, Job through the Song of Solomon, are usually called the Wisdom Literature. Job was at one time considered to be the oldest book in the Bible, but best modern scholarship places the writing at around 500 B.C.E., certainly after the great prophets.

Job is drama, poetry, dialogue. It asks a central question, "Why do the righteous suffer?" and a couple of related ones, such as: "Does religion pay off?" and "Why was I born?" Job is set in a very ancient frame: God and Satan are together, and God is boasting about Job, who never steps out of line, worships in sincerity, and so on. Satan sneers at all this and why not? Nothing bad has ever happened to Job. He's wealthy with great flocks and herds. He has a large and successful family. He is healthy. Why wouldn't he praise God? So God agrees to a test; Satan can take Job's wealth and family from him.

In a very short space of time, all of Job's livestock is stolen, struck by lightning or what have you, so that he is bankrupt. A tornado hits the house where his children are at a dinner, and they are all killed. To all this Job responds, "The LORD gave, and the LORD hath taken away; Blessed be the name of the LORD" (1:21). So, the first round goes to God. But Satan says, in effect, "Yes—but his health. That's the acid test." Talleyrand, minister of France, said something like "I cannot worry about the fate of the world today—I have a blister on my heel." If one feels good physically, many things can be taken in stride. So God agrees that Job's health is also in Satan's hands, and Job is made miserable with sore boils from head to foot. Most scholars equate this with a particularly painful type of leprosy. All he has left is his wife, and apparently this is not an unmixed blessing. All she can find to say to her suffering husband is "curse God, and die" (2:9).

Job never curses God, but he does curse the day he was born. The person who coined the phrase "the patience of Job" apparently didn't read beyond the second chapter, for Job becomes very impatient indeed, especially when his three friends(?) supposedly come to offer comfort. They insist that his tragedies must be the result of great sin on his part. Job vehemently denies this and craves more than anything else a chance to plead his case before Jehovah. The current feeling in Job's day was that all suffering was the result of sin—if not the sin of the sufferer, then the sin of his forebears.

This same thought prevailed in Jesus' time. Remember when the disciples asked Jesus about the man born blind: "Who sinned—this man or his parents?" Jesus' reply was that neither the man nor his parents were responsible. I think any honest assessment has to come to the conclusion that often suffering is caused by sin, one's own or another's. However, often it is not.

Job expresses for most of us bewilderment at the injustice we see, and perhaps a sneaking suspicion that we could have managed things better! Job is never given an answer as such to his insistent "Why?" What he is given is a new concept of God and a new relationship with God. In the end, Job seems to accept the fact that he is the creature of a sovereign God, and that he cannot understand the might, the majesty, the mind of God. This is my comfort in the insoluble problems raised by the Bible and by the world in which we live. If I could understand the mind, the majesty, and the purpose of God, what would I need with him?

Many notable verses and much beautiful poetry is found in Job such as,

"Though he slay me, yet will I trust in him" (13:15);
"Oh that I knew where I might find him!" (23:3);
"Where wast thou when I laid the foundations of the earth?" (38:4);
"KNOWEST thou the time when the wild goats . . . bring forth?" (39:1).

And many more. It deserves individual study, though it is not an easy book.

Psalms

The book of Psalms is the hymnbook of Israel—the faith of a people set to music. These songs were written over a long period of time, perhaps 1000-200 B.C.E., and by a number of different people, many undoubtedly by David. Most of them were intended either for public worship or for private devotions. There are themes of praise, repentance, despair, love, hate, joy, sorrow, vengeance. However, the dominant theme is praise. Of course, some of the most magnificent words in the Bible are found in this collection. The 22nd, which most scholars think Christ was quoting from the cross, "My God, my God, why hast thou forsaken me?" (v. 1) and that Jesus may have silently continued in his thoughts to include v. 27: "All the ends of the world shall remember and turn unto the LORD." The 23rd is perhaps the best known of any Old Testament chapter. The 24th, the 46th, and the 51st, as mentioned before, are David's cry of confession and repentance. The lofty 90th and the 91st, quoted by Satan at the time of Christ's temptations in the wilderness. The 119th, much the longest. The confident, joyous 121st and 122nd. The 137th, a psalm of the captivity whose latter verses are frightening in their vindictiveness. The magnificent 139th, Francis Thompson's inspiration for his "Hound of Heaven." And finally, the last, the 150th:

Praise ye the LORD.

Praise God in his sanctuary:

praise him in the firmament of his power.

Praise him for his mighty acts:

praise him according to his excellent greatness.

Praise him with the sound of the trumpet:

praise him with the psaltery and harp.

Praise him with the timbrel and dance:

praise him with stringed instruments and organs.

Praise him upon the loud cymbals:

praise him upon the high sounding cymbals:

Let every thing that hath breath praise the LORD.

Praise ye the LORD."

I am always possessed by an overwhelming desire to quote that one when I hear somebody breathing indignation about the use of guitars, for example, in a Sunday service. Psalms is a book with something for every mood, and the Christian who is not intimately familiar with it misses a lot.

Proverbs

Proverbs is something of a comedown after the music of Psalms. It is philosophy rather than poetry, and some of it is moralizing, pedantic, and boring. But there is also much wisdom, common sense, and humor in it. It is a collection of sayings, maxims, and, of course, proverbs.

Most families along the line have acquired their own sayings that have special meaning in certain situations, and some of the biblical ones are close to that level. For instance, a favorite in our family is, "If it ain't broke, don't fix it!" which, by stretching a point, might have some kinship with 26:17: "He that . . . meddleth with strife *belonging* not to him, *is like* one that taketh a dog by the ears."

There are a number concerning domestic tranquillity:

"A continual dropping in a very rainy day and a contentious woman are alike" (27:15).

"*It is* better to dwell in a corner of the housetop, than with a brawling woman in a wide house" (21:9).

There are a great many more about troublesome women than their male counterparts, but then, these were written by men. Traditionally, a number of them were written by Solomon, who understandably had women trouble, since he had saddled himself with so many females to cope with.

A number are of a somewhat higher level. They include:

"A friend loveth at all times, and a brother is born for adversity" (17:17);

"Pride *goeth* before destruction, and an haughty spirit before a fall" (16:18).

"TRUST in the LORD with all thine heart; and lean not unto thine own understanding" (3:5).

"HAPPY *is* the man *that* findeth wisdom" (3:13).

"A FALSE balance *is* abomination to the LORD" (11:1).

"Better *is* little with the fear of the LORD, than great treasure and trouble therewith. Better *is* a dinner of herbs where love is, than a stalled ox and hatred therewith" (15:16, 17).

"To do justice and judgment *is* more acceptable to the LORD than sacrifice" (21:3).

"A *GOOD* name *is* rather to be chosen than great riches" (22:1).

And a great many more.

If there is an overall philosophy to be discerned, it is that those who behave wisely and righteously will prosper and those who don't will suffer. The two passages that I find most poetic are these:

"There be three *things which* are too wonderful for me, yea, four which I know not: The way of an eagle in the air; the way of a serpent upon a rock; the way of a ship in the midst of the sea; and the way of a man with a maid" (30:18, 19).

And then the closing part of the book, the familiar verses beginning "Who can find a virtuous woman? For her price *is* far above rubies" (31:10)—most often chosen as the Scripture for Mother's Day. Read it again and continue to read until the end of the book, and you will find that women's lib was not unknown back then. The woman extolled in the final chapter of Proverbs was a career girl as well as a homemaker, and also did volunteer work.

By and large, Proverbs is a book for dipping into rather than reading chapter by chapter. It can be delightful and rewarding.

Ecclesiastes, or the Preacher

If I had to pick five books of the Bible that I could do without, Ecclesiastes would be one of them. On the whole it is cynical, skeptical, and pessimistic: "For what hath man of all his labour .... For all his days *are* sorrows" (2:22, 23). Or how about this one: "I have seen all the works that are done under the sun; and, behold, all *is* vanity and vexation of spirit" (1:14). Or, "the race *is* not to the swift, nor the battle to the strong, . . . but time and chance happeneth to them all" (9:11).

Some of the book is similar to Proverbs, but it is much more dolorous. For instance, Ecclesiastes 9:3 reads, "... the heart of the sons of men is full of evil, and madness *is* in their heart while they live, and after that *they* go to the dead."

There are two familiar and rather beautiful passages, however. In the third chapter, the first eight verses begin:

To every *thing there is* a season,
and a time to every purpose under the heaven:
A time to be born, and a time to die;
a time to plant, and a time to pluck up *that which is* planted;
A time to kill, and a time to heal;
a time to break down, and a time to build up;
A time to weep, and a time to laugh;
a time to mourn, and a time to dance;
A time to cast away stones, and a time to gather stones together;
a time to embrace, and a time to refrain from embracing;
A time to get, and a time to lose;
a time to keep, and a time to cast away;
A time to rend, and a time to sew;
a time to keep silence, and a time to speak;
A time to love, and a time to hate;
a time of war, and a time of peace. (3:1–8)

Also the first seven verses of the last chapter are beautiful:

Remember now thy Creator in the days of thy youth,
while the evil days come not,
nor the years draw nigh, when thou shalt say,
I have no pleasure in them;
While the sun, or the light, or the moon,
or the stars, be not darkened,
nor the clouds return after the rain:
In the day when the keepers of the house shall tremble,
and the strong men shall bow themselves,
and the grinders cease because they are few,
And those that look out of the windows be darkened,
And the doors shall be shut in the streets,
when the sound of the grinding is low,
and he shall rise up at the voice of the bird,
and all the daughters of music shall be brought low;
Also *when* they shall be afraid of *that which is* high,
and fears *shall be* in the way,
and the almond tree shall flourish,
and the grasshopper shall be a burden,
and desire shall fail:

because man goeth to his long home,
and the mourners go about the streets:
Or ever the silver cord be loosed,
or the golden bowl be broken,
or the pitcher be broken at the fountain,
or the wheel broken at the cistern.
Then shall the dust return to the earth as it was:
and the spirit shall return unto God who gave it.

(12:1-7)

The conclusion the Preacher reaches seems to be that the world is full of trouble, inconsistencies, and mystery, and that humankind's part is to "Fear God, and keep his commandments: for this *is* the whole *duty* of man" (12:13).

The Song of Solomon

The Song of Solomon is a beautiful love poem that had trouble making it into the canon because it was considered too sensual. In order to include it, the rabbis came up with an allegorical interpretation: Israel was the bride, and Yahweh her lover. Later the Christian church decided that the church was the bride and Christ her lover. This is one of the places in the Bible where I (with the support of most modern scholars) prefer to take the book at its face value as a beautiful love song, probably sung at village weddings. There are many places where the Bible celebrates the sexual love between a man and woman, and I think this is one of them. While Solomon's name is given to it, it seems more likely that it dates from considerably after his time, at around 300 B.C.E. Also it sounds like a much franker and simpler relationship than a sophisticated harem owner would be likely to extol. At any rate, I'm glad we weren't cheated of:

For lo, the winter is past,
the rain is over *and* gone;
The flowers appear on the earth;
the time of the singing *of birds* is come,
and the voice of the turtle is heard in our land;
The fig tree putteth forth her green figs,
and the vines *with* the tender grape give a *good* smell.

Arise, my love, my fair one, and come away.

(2:11-13)

"I *am* my beloved, and my beloved *is* mine" (6:3). Or, "for love *is* strong as death; jealousy *is* cruel as the grave .... Many waters cannot quench love, neither can floods drown it" (8:6, 7).

7

The Prophets

*T*he remaining seventeen books in the Old Testament are books of prophecy, and a profound study in themselves, of course. The writing prophets, Isaiah through Malachi, cover about five hundred years, about 750–250 B.C.E. (and with at least the latter part of Daniel considerably after that, around 165 B.C.E.). Let us not forget, however, that prophecy was important to the Jews long before that in the persons of Samuel, Nathan, Elijah, and Elisha, to mention only a few.

What was the purpose of the prophet? To foretell the future? Only incidentally. I like what Neil has to say about the prophets:

> Some were more articulate and some more fanatical than others. All of them claimed to be speaking on behalf of God, and none of them regarded the faith of Israel as a meditative pursuit to be engaged in within the cloister or the study but as something to be proclaimed, defended and fought for in the political and social stresses of his day. 'Keeping politics out of the pulpit' was the last thing any prophet ever dreamt of doing.[1]

Among these prophets and within their collected works are to be found the persons and the ideas that moulded Israel's faith and prepared the way for the coming of Christ and the institution of his church.

Isaiah

Isaiah is probably the most important of the prophetic books and certainly the one most quoted in the New Testament. It has long been considered to be the work of at least two authors, and a good deal of

[1]From *Harper's Bible Commentary,* by William Neil. Copyright © 1962 by Hodder & Stoughton Ltd. New York: Harper & Row, 1962, p. 241.

modern criticism postulates a third. The man for whom it is named and who is responsible for the first thirty-nine chapters was a native of Jerusalem and prophesied in Judah at about the same time Amos and Hosea were prophesying in Israel. A part of Isaiah's mission is during the reign of Hezekiah. Isaiah is a prophet convinced of the awesome holiness of the Lord, and yet sure of his love and of the coming of a Messiah.

There are many well-loved passages in this first portion:

Come now, and let us reason together,
saith the LORD:
though your sins be as scarlet,
they shall be as white as snow (1:18).

And he shall judge among the nations,
and shall rebuke many people:
and they shall beat their swords into plowshares,
and their spears into pruning hooks:
nation shall not lift up sword against nation,
neither shall they learn war any more (2:4).

For unto us a child is born,
unto us a son is given:
and the government shall be upon his shoulder:
and his name shall be called
Wonderful, Counseler, The mighty God,
The everlasting Father, The Prince of Peace (9:6).

Say to them *that are* of a fearful heart,
Be strong, fear not:
behold, your God will come *with* vengeance,
even God *with* a recompense;
he will come and save you.
Then the eyes of the blind shall be opened,
and the ears of the deaf shall be unstopped.
Then shall the lame *man* leap as an hart,
and the tongue of the dumb sing:
for in the wilderness shall waters break out,
and streams in the desert (35:4–6).

Second Isaiah, chs. 40—55 (or 40 to the end of the book) was written during and/or after the exile, depending on which part you are reading. It, too, has beautiful and familiar material:

COMFORT ye, comfort ye my people,
Saith your God. (40:1)

Every valley shall be exalted,
and every mountain and hill shall be made low:
and the crooked shall be made straight,
and the rough places plain (40:4).

He shall feed his flock like a shepherd:
he shall gather the lambs with his arm,
and carry *them* in his bosom,
and shall gently lead those that are with young (40:11);

HO, every one that thirsteth, come ye to the waters,
and he that hath no money;
come ye, buy, and eat; Yea, come, buy wine and milk
without money and without price (55:1);

ARISE, shine; for thy light is come,
and the glory of the LORD has risen upon thee (60:1).

THE Spirit of the Lord GOD *is* upon me;
because the LORD hath anointed me
to preach good tidings unto the meek;
he hath sent me to bind up the broken-hearted,
to proclaim liberty to the captives,
and the opening of the prison to *them that are bound;*
To proclaim the acceptable year of the LORD,
and the day of vengeance of our God;
to comfort all that mourn;
To appoint unto them that mourn in Zion,
to give unto them beauty for ashes,
the oil of joy for mourning,
the garment of praise for the spirit of heaviness;
that they might be called trees of righteousness,
the planting of LORD, that he might be glorified (61:1-3).

I suppose no one who has heard Handel's *Messiah* can read Isaiah without remembering the thrill of those glorious passages set to glorious music.

Jeremiah

Jeremiah is very different, and for the average reader, far inferior to Isaiah. It is full of denunciation and discouragement. Yet Jeremiah is an important figure, for he tells more of the last days of Judah than any other writer. He is an unpopular prophet, for he says things the people do not want to hear. He is imprisoned and persecuted. Yet along with all his devastating predictions, there is hope in Jeremiah, for he says that eventually the Lord will make a new covenant with Israel and Judah:

"But this *shall be* the covenant that I will make with the house of Israel; After those days, saith the LORD, I will put my law in their inward parts, and write it in their hearts; and will be their God, and they shall be my people" (31:33).

Lamentations

Lamentations is a book of five poems or hymns about the fall of Jerusalem to Babylon. The poems were for a long time ascribed to Jeremiah; however, most criticism now thinks they were not written by him, though the timing would fit. They are full of grief and sorrow, yet also full of faith. The most familiar verse is probably, "*IS it* nothing to you, all ye that pass by? behold, and see if there be any sorrow like unto my sorrow" (1:12). The last two verses express the book's tone: "Turn thou us unto thee, O LORD, and we shall be turned; renew our days as of old. But thou hast utterly rejected us; thou art very wroth against us" (5:21–22).

Ezekiel

The prophet Ezekiel was deported with the first batch of exiles. Neil says that

> had it not been for prophets of the stature of Jeremiah, Ezekiel and Second Isaiah, who convinced enough people

that the sack of Jerusalem and the Exile were the voice of God speaking through history, the pageant of Israel's story would have ended in a whimper beside the canals of Mesopotamia. Such was not the will of God, however, and we have seen in the dirges of *Lamentations* how the true prophetic word infiltrated into common thought through the liturgy, and hope for the future replaced despair.[2]

Ezekiel, unlike Isaiah and Jeremiah, begins at the beginning and ends at the end. From his call in 592 B.C.E. to the fall of Jerusalem in 587 B.C.E., he preached judgment and repentance. However, from 587 to 570 B.C.E., he was a consoler and reformer. Ezekiel's book is full of symbolism. The two most familiar examples are the valley of dry bones and the wheel, inspirations for two well-known spirituals, "dem bones gonna rise again" and "Ezekiel saw de wheel way up in de middle of de air." Also in Ezekiel, we get the doctrine of individual responsibility plainly spelled out and a negation of blaming the fathers for the sins of the children (see 18:1-9).

Daniel

Daniel, if read superficially, can be subject to some pretty wild interpretations. The first half of Daniel has more narrative than any of the other prophetic books except Jonah, which is almost totally narrative. This first half contains six stories dealing with the Hebrew captives (especially Daniel) in the Babylonian court, though most scholars feel that the book was written long after the captivity, probably around 167 B.C.E.

Chapter 1 is a temperance tale. Chapter 2 is an interpretation of Nebuchahnezzar's dream. Chapter 3 is the story of the Hebrew children Shadrach, Meshach, and Abednego in the fiery furnace. In chapter 4, there are more dreams. Chapter 5 deals with Belshazzar's feast and the handwriting on the wall. And chapter 6 is about Daniel in the lions' den.

If we accept the 167 B.C.E. date, this would tie in with the persecutions under Antiochus, in intertestamental times, and how these stories of steadfastness in the face of danger were set down to

---

[2]From *Harper's Bible Commentary*, by William Neil, p. 262.

encourage the people of the later date to faithfulness. The latter part of the book is strange, obscure, apocalyptic, and eschatological (meaning last things), with a lot of resemblance to Revelation. And, like Revelation, the book of Daniel lends itself to all sorts of wild interpretations.

It is easier reading if one bears in mind the things that were happening to the Jews just before the Maccabean revolt—of which I will say more later. Daniel 12:8 reads, "And I heard, but I understood not: then said I, O my Lord, what *shall be* the end of these *things?*" which pretty well expresses my feelings about the last half of the book.

Hosea

When we get to Hosea we are back some two centuries before the events in the first half of Daniel—the last days of the Northern Kingdom, around 740 B.C.E. Hosea is a beautiful book, full of the love and mercy of God, in an allegorical frame of Hosea's marriage to a harlot. She bears him three children and leaves him to go back to her former life. She sinks to the very bottom; yet Hosea buys her back and gives her another chance. So with God and his erring children.

Hosea paints a clear picture of a morally decadent people going down to inevitable ruin. The theme is well expressed in 13:9: "O ISRAEL, thou hast destroyed thyself; but in me *is* thine help," and 14:4:"I WILL heal their backsliding, I will love them freely . . . ." And in 6:6:"For I desired mercy, and not sacrifice; And the knowledge of God more than burnt offerings." Our familiar saying about sowing the wind and reaping the whirlwind is found in 8:7:"For they have sown the wind, and they shall reap the whirlwind: it hath no stalk: the bud shall yield no meal: if so be it yield, the strangers shall swallow it up."

Joel

Joel is difficult and comparatively unimportant alongside such greats as Amos and Hosea. Joel is a prophet in Judah, with the date uncertain. Some scholars say as early as 800 B.C.E., but more believe the dates are as late as 400 B.C.E. Joel talks about the "day of the Lord," and both judgment and mercy are foretold. The most familiar verse is probably 2:28:

And it shall come to pass afterward,
that I will pour out my spirit upon all flesh;
and your sons and your daughters shall prophesy,
your old men shall dream dreams,
your young men shall see visions.

Amos

Amos appeared in the Northern Kingdom of Israel about the middle of the eighth century, some twenty years before Hosea. (The arrangement of the books in the Bible could be improved upon.) Amos is the prophet of God's righteousness and of social justice. The social gospel is nothing new to our day. Amos and Hosea both preached it fervently and condemned "going through the motions" of religion, certainly another reason, if any is needed, to the relevancy of Scriptures. The great gap between rich and poor was as real then as it is today, and it troubled Amos to the core. "Woe to them *that are* at ease in Zion" (6:1).

I hate, I despise your feast days,
and I will not smell in your solemn assemblies.
Though ye offer me burnt offerings and your meat offerings,
I will not accept *them:*
neither will I regard the peace offerings of your fat beasts.
Take thou away from the noise of thy songs;
for I will not hear the melody of thy viols.
But let judgment run down as waters,
and righteousness as a mighty stream.   (5:21-24)

Obadiah

Obadiah is the shortest book in the Old Testament, and probably the least important. It contains one chapter of twenty-one verses. Nothing is really known about Obadiah or his date. He pronounces judgment upon Edom (this is probably after the exile, and Edom was a rival of the Jewish nation). Notable quotes from this book are: "The pride of thine heart hath deceived thee" (1:3), and "the kingdom shall be the LORD's" (1:21).

Jonah

Jonah is different. Rather than a collection of the prophet's utterances, it is about the man himself. Yet the drama, while fascinating, is not the point at all. It really doesn't matter whether you want to take the book as allegory or whether you prefer to argue that, in the providence of God, it was possible for a man to be swallowed by a great fish and survive the ordeal. This is not a story about a whale. It is a magnificent account of God's attempt to convince an intransigent bigot, Jonah, that the love and grace of God are for all people, even the nasty Ninevehites.

Jonah acted out childish attempts to thwart God's mercy. The unknown writer is trying very hard to convince the Jewish people (almost certainly after the return from exile, when the community had become exclusive, rigid, and convinced that the Hebrews alone were to be the recipients of Jehovah's grace) that there was room in God's love for all of humanity.

Perhaps the most notable quote is from chapter 4, "for I knew that thou *art* a gracious God, and merciful, slow to anger, and of great kindness" (v. 2), because while Jonah did know all this, he kept hoping against hope that somehow these qualities could be reserved for upright Israelites.

The story ends with a question from God, asking Jonah if he wanted even the children and the flocks of Nineveh destroyed: "And should not I spare Nineveh, that great city, wherein are more than sixscore thousand persons that cannot discern between their right hand and their left hand; and *also* much cattle?" (4:11). We are not given Jonah's answer. Did he finally relent and come around to God's way of thinking?

Micah

Micah was a prophet to Judah and probably a contemporary of 1 Isaiah. However, Micah was more concerned with the common people than with the leaders and national policy. Like Amos and Hosea, Micah rails against injustice and lip-service religion. This is summed up magnificently in the well-loved verse: ". . . what doth the LORD require of thee, but to do justly, and to love mercy, and to walk humbly with thy God?" (6:8). He is also the prophet who foretells that the Messiah is to be born in Bethlehem and that "[n]ation shall not lift up a sword against nation, neither shall they learn war any more" (4:3).

Nahum

Nahum is a hymn of vengeful rejoicing over the downfall of Assyria and Nineveh in 612 B.C.E. with no word of pity for the vanquished, but with some tremendous tributes to the power of Jehovah. Certainly Nahum is one of the lesser prophetic books, so we'll move on.

Habakkuk

There is considerable question as to the date of Habakkuk. It could be as early as 600 B.C.E., not long before the fall of Judah. Or it could possibly be in the intertestamental period when Alexander the Great was overrunning the world. The message is the same in either case. Habakkuk is a questioning prophet. He can see that the sins of Judah merit destruction and that God uses the heathen as an instrument of it. But then the heathen are worse than Judah, so what about them?

God's answer is that they shall not escape. Habakkuk's words about injustice are reminiscent of Amos and Hosea. The most notable quote is in Habakkuk 2:4: "the just shall live by his faith," a startling forerunner of Paul's words in Romans 1:17: "For therein is the righteousness of God revealed from faith to faith: at it is written, The just shall live by faith"—the words that transformed Luther's life. Habakkuk is a call to wholehearted commitment—and to trust when understanding is difficult.

Zephaniah

Zephaniah was a prophet in Judah not long before its fall, probably in the early days of King Josiah before any of his reforms could have taken effect. It is a picture of gloom and despair, and, like Joel, the prophet foretells the "day of the Lord" when wickedness will be punished. Yet there is still a note of hope. After that terrible day, salvation will eventually come:

> The Lord thy God in the midst of thee *is* mighty;
> he will save, he will rejoice over thee with joy;

he will rest in his love,
he will joy over thee with singing. (3:17)

Haggai

Haggai is from a different period, after the exile, when the remnant has returned to the Holy City. Most of the two chapters is devoted to urging the people to complete the restoration of the Temple, which was sorely needed by the returned exiles to strengthen their religious life. Even more glorious than Solomon's great Temple:

"The glory of this latter house shall be greater than the former, saith the LORD of hosts: and in this place will I give peace, saith the LORD of hosts" (2:9).

Zechariah

Zechariah was a contemporary of Haggai's, with much the same point of view, but a less straightforward way of presenting it, and with a number of obscure apocalyptic visions. He was also a Messianic prophet, and foretells the Palm Sunday processional:

REJOICE greatly, O daughter of Zion;
shout, O daughter of Jerusalem: behold, thy King cometh unto
    thee:
he *is* just, and having salvation;
lowly, and riding upon an ass,
and upon a colt the foal of an ass. (9:9)

And, he also mentions the thirty pieces of silver: "And I said unto them, If ye think good, give *me* my price; and if not, forbear. So they weighed for my price thirty *pieces* of silver" (11:12).

This is a difficult book to make sense of, but there is a lot of hope in it, as well as an obsession with ritualistic holiness such as in the following verses:

"And the LORD shall be King over all the earth: in that day shall there be one LORD, and his name one" (14:9).

"In that day shall there be upon the bells of the horses, HOLINESS UNTO THE LORD; and the pots in the LORD's house shall be like the bowls before the altar" (14:20).

Malachi

Malachi is of the same general period as the last two: a postexilic prophet to Judah, probably shortly before the coming of Nehemiah and his ambitious program. The people are being neglectful of religious practice and are guilty of immorality. They are not even supporting the temple worship financially:

> Bring ye all the tithes into the storehouse,
> that there may be meat in mine house,
> and prove me now herewith,
> saith the LORD of hosts,
> if I will not open you the windows of heaven,
> and pour you out a blessing, that *there shall* not *be room* enough
> *to receive it.* (3:10) (often used in stewardship sermons, naturally).

Another familiar quote:

> But unto you that fear my name
> shall the Sun of righteousness arise with healing in his wings;
> and ye shall go forth, and grow up as calves of the stall. (4:2)

And so with Malachi, we come to the end of the prophetic writings.

How does one sum up the message of the prophets? They spoke for God to the people, bluntly and boldly. They warned of the consequences of sin—individual and national. They foretold suffering, but they also spoke of hope and of faith. And above all, they preached the greatness of the Lord: Shape up, or you'll be in trouble. Yet God loves his people and is a mighty and a steadfast Jehovah.

Without the prophets, who can venture a guess as to what the community of Christ's time would have been? A modern preacher would appreciate this very lament (though I don't remember where I heard it):

> We'd like to speak out brave and bold,
> as prophets did in days of old;
> but we depend for bread and butter
> on those who hear the words we utter.
> When Amos and Hosea spoke
> they wore no congregation's yoke.

8

Between the Testaments

When we reach the end of the Old Testament with the last verse of Malachi, we are at about the year 400 B.C.E., give or take a half century in either direction. As I mentioned before, it is very difficult to be precise about a lot of biblical dates. This time of approximately 400 B.C.E. has to do with the events themselves, not the recording of them. Some of the recording was done probably as late as 150 B.C.E., but let's say for an end of the Old Testament story that the date was 400 B.C.E.

The New Testament opens around 4 B.C.E. So, you may ask, what happened to the world and to the Hebrews during those four centuries? I mentioned that Neil saw the Bible as drama with most of the Old Testament as Act 1, followed by the prologue, and with the four Gospels comprising Act 2. For my part, I would suggest the intertestamental period as the intermission. We have no canonical record of those years, but there were many Jewish writings, some of them preserved in the Apocrypha (the fourteen books found between the testaments in the Catholic Bible and in many pulpit Bibles). There is also, of course, a great deal of secular history of those years, as cataclysmic things were happening.

When the Old Testament story ends, Persia has conquered Babylon, and the Jewish community back in Jerusalem is a vassal state. When the New Testament opens, Rome is very much in the driver's seat, and the Jews are subject to Roman rule. What has gone on in between?

Well, Persia continued to rule the Near East for more than two hundred years until Philip of Macedon came on the scene. In 338 B.C.E., he controlled all of Greece. His son, Alexander the Great, went far beyond his father's ambition, and in 333 B.C.E., he conquered Persia. Two years later, by 331 B.C.E., he had conquered the world of his day and wept beside the Indus River because there were no more worlds to conquer. A story is told of him that shows rare perception in such a young and powerful figure. It appears that he had one slave whose only duty was to follow him around and murmur at intervals, "Sire, remember. Thou art mortal!" With Alexander, the Greek period came firmly into being: The Greek language, culture, and, to some extent, religion became the order of the day. At the time of Christ, while the power was Roman, a great deal of Greek influence remained. For example, Greek was still the literary language, which explains why the New Testament was not written in Latin, the language of Rome.

Alexander's meteoric career lasted for only twelve years. He died of a fever in 323 B.C.E., at the age of thirty-two. He had no heir and, for years, a number of his generals fought over the empire. Finally it was divided into Macedonia, Egypt, and Syria. Palestine was something of a political football, first under Egypt and then annexed to Syria. Because our interest is solely in the little patch of Palestine where the Jewish community of law exists, I am oversimplifying, leaving out a lot. Suffice it to say, it was a complicated period with a lot of jockeying for power. Also during this time a lot of the Jews were scattered to various parts of the empire, notably to Alexandria in North Africa. The Jews suffered a number of indignities at the hands of Syria. It was not until 175 B.C.E., when Antiochus, also known as Epiphanes, ascended the throne of Syria (albeit with a vassal-type arrangement with Rome) that things became unbearable.

Antiochus was determined to unify his domain and believed that the Grecian way of life and thought was the most unifying force he had handy. He attempted to force the Jews to worship the Greek god Zeus, going so far as to have a statue of him set up in the Holy of Holies in the Temple. Circumcision, the covenant rite, and Sabbath observance were forbidden. Finally a devout Jew by the name of Mattathias was ordered, in 167 B.C.E., to sacrifice to Zeus on an altar set up in the Temple at Jerusalem. He refused and killed the king's official who was present. He and his five sons fled into the hills and began an ambitious program of guerilla warfare. Mattathias died the next year, but one of his sons, Judas Maccabeus, known as "the hammer," took over command of the guerilla forces. Judas Maccabeus was such a successful leader that the Jews won out against Syria, retook Jerusalem, removed all the pagan trappings from the Temple, and in 164 B.C.E. rededicated it. The Feast of Purification and Dedication harks back to this as well as to the book of Esther. The Jews then, under the Maccabees and their descendants, had a measure of freedom, self-rule, and prosperity for about a century until in 63 B.C.E. Jerusalem was subdued by the Roman general Pompey. Judea then became subject to Rome. None of this is in the Bible, but some is in the Apocrypha.

At the birth of Christ, the Jews have been Roman subjects for about a generation and find the hand of the conqueror heavy. Rome was not an easy place in which to be a Christian. There are still plenty of rebels among the Hebrews, especially a group known as the Zealots. Some scholars think Judas Iscariot belonged to their number.

For three centuries, before the birth of Christ, there was a growing cosmopolitanism. Persia paved the way, but Alexander brought it into being. He and his successors and the Romans encouraged the founding and growth of cities. For a considerable period before Christ's coming, there was unrest and disillusionment about life in general. In the Greek or Gentile world, there was a changing standard of ethics, the rise of intellectualism, moral decay, a great gap between rich and poor, lavish display, infanticide, abortion, cruelty to slaves (every third person on the streets of Rome was a slave), disregard of marriage ties, bald obscenity on the stage, brutal slaughter in the arena. For the masses, life was little more than a mixture of despair and resignation, lightened by the countless diversions (for example, the arena games) designed to lessen their discontent.

The philosophers looked for some clue to give a meaning to life. The two major groups were the Stoics, who believed that blind acceptance of whatever happens is the only answer, with suicide a worthy way out if things got too tough. The Epicureans, on the other hand, considered happiness the goal of life, with satisfaction of the senses as the best way of escape. Eat, drink, be merry—a cop-out as far as the problems of the world were concerned.

This was the Gentile world. It was a world, certainly, in a surprising way ready for the coming of Christ. In a material sense, there was now a unified language: Greek. There were, under the Romans, better travel conditions than had ever existed before. And, by and large, the people were living in more settled communities. In a spiritual sense, as mentioned above, there was a hunger—a feeling of lack; a search for something better. So "in the fullness of time," God sent his Son.

What of the restricted, law-burdened, exclusivist world of the Hebrews? Well, when the New Testament opens, the Temple at Jerusalem is still their lifeblood. Pilgrims from all parts of the empire would make their way there to celebrate the Passover, the Day of Atonement, to pay their vows, and to draw near to God. The high priest and the Sanhedrin, under the authority of the Roman government, exercised surprising power over the life of the people. The Sadducees, comprising the privileged priesthood, supported the high priest in a somewhat uneasy liaison with the more popular lay party of the Pharisees, the pillars of the law, who were often hypocritical but were religious and patriotic. The Sadducees were probably more sophisticated and more open to the Greek way of life.

There were also the Essenes, a monkish, ascetic sect (you will no doubt remember that it was in the ruins of an Essene community where the Dead Sea Scrolls were discovered), and the previously mentioned Zealots, a nationalistic party probably a holdover from the Maccabees. These two were small groups. And then, of course, there was the great mass of the common people struggling to obey the law, wrestling a living that would keep them alive after the heavy bite of the Roman taxes, and sending their children to the synagogue schools and hoping that life for them would be better. They were looking for a Messiah whom the prophets had foretold, and who would strike off the yoke of the Gentile conquerors.

At this time, four institutions were extremely important in Jewish life: the Temple at Jerusalem; the local synagogue, the center of day-by-day worship; the law, which by this time affected almost every detail of daily living and had become almost a god in itself; and finally the Sanhedrin, the Jewish governing body of 71 elders, holding their positions through heredity, with the high priest at their head. The Sanhedrin was the supreme court of the Jews and the final court of appeal under Rome, handling all judicial matters not reserved for officers of the empire. Rome was inclined to give its subjects a fair amount of local freedom as long as two conditions prevailed. First, that the taxes came in on time and in full, and second, that nobody made waves—no riots and whatnot to be put down.

With the Sanhedrin handling a great many judicial matters, there was certainly no separation, on the local level, of church and state. The Sanhedrin could arrest, imprison, and have miscreants flogged. It had its own temple guard of soldiers. In a trial, if the prisoner was acquitted, it would usually be announced the same day. If condemned, not until the following day. It took a simple majority for acquittal, but a two-thirds vote for conviction. A death sentence pronounced by the body had to be ratified and carried out by the Roman authorities. Otherwise, Jesus would not have been taken before Pilate.

At the birth of Jesus, Herod the Great, half Hebrew by birth, Jewish by religion (at least nominally), but Greek in his sympathies, ruled Palestine under Rome, from 27 B.C.E. to 4 B.C.E. It was Herod, you'll no doubt recall, who encountered the wise men and who ordered the massacre of the infants. His three sons inherited the kingdom: Philip had the area around Caesarea Philippi and was a reasonably good ruler for some thirty years; Herod Antipas was tetrarch of Galilee and Peraea for about forty years and is the Herod most frequently mentioned in the New Testament and the one who had John the Baptist put to death; and there was Archelaus who ruled Judea, Samaria, and Idumaea badly for about ten years and then was replaced by a Roman procurator.

9

The Gospels:
The Life of Christ

*T*he four Gospels constitute what Neil calls Act 2 of the biblical drama. The word *gospel* can well be translated "good news," and these four books are full of it. In a sense, the Old Testament is a record of failure: Men and women throughout its pages were given chance after chance at God's love and grace. They sinned, were warned, were punished, repented, and were given another chance— and then the whole sorry cycle began anew. God tried again and again with love, forgiveness, disaster, the prophets, the captivity to bring his people to total love for and commitment to him. The good news of the Gospels is that God tried one last time, with a sacrifice that staggers human understanding, in the sending of Jesus Christ.

Matthew, Mark, Luke, and John tell essentially the same story—a story of Christ's birth, ministry, death, and resurrection. Each writer had a different point of view, a different purpose, and wrote for a different set of people. The first three, called the Synoptics, have a good deal in common. Mark was written first, almost certainly, and is much the shortest. Both Matthew and Luke contain considerable material that is in Mark, and they also have material in common that is not in Mark. A lot of Matthew is not found in either Mark or Luke, and Luke has a considerable amount that is not in Matthew or Mark. John, probably written much later than the other three, has little material that is found in them with only about 8 percent of duplication. Remember that these books were written at least thirty years after the events they recount took place.

Though the Gospels are first in the New Testament, they were not written first. Some of Paul's letters claim that place. They are a combination of accounts of eyewitnesses, material from sermons used in the early church, collections of sayings, and, on occasion, editorial comments. No original document for any biblical book exists, as far as is known. (There may be a very good reason for this. What a temptation to worship a scrap of parchment!) Also remember that there was no printed matter in that day. Scrolls were scarce and very costly, and people depended much more upon their memory than we do in our "make a note" day. A great deal of schooling was simply practice in rote memory.

As to why the books were not written earlier, at first the disciples were very busy coping with many other things, and it was all so clear in their own minds that there probably seemed no need for a written record. It is also important to realize that most of the early Christians looked for Christ's return in the imminent future. It was only as they slowly came to a realization that perhaps this was not to be that a written record became of paramount importance. They saw the eyewitnesses dying off. They also saw that as the far-flung churches were increasing, they urgently needed reliable information, doctrine, and the recording of what Christ had done and said. There are innumerable testimonies as to the reliability of the Gospel records, from both religious and secular sources.

Now for the books themselves. Matthew is traditionally ascribed to the Matthew of the twelve apostles—the renegade tax collector for the hated conquerors. There are arguments as to how much of the book can actually be attributed to Matthew and how much comes from collections then current of Jesus' teachings. However, this sort of biblical criticism would demand a much longer and more exhaustive treatment than concerns us here. It is perhaps worth pointing out that authorship was looked at differently in those days. It was considered a compliment, for example, for a follower to put the name of his teacher on his own writings. (This very likely happened with 2 Peter.) Also, plagiarism was considered more as praise than as theft. In any case, the author of Matthew was a Jewish Christian, writing for fellow Jews and bent on convincing them that Jesus was the Messiah foretold by the Old Testament Prophets.

Matthew also emphasizes the kingly Christ, the Messianic King. It is notable that Matthew, in one of the two birth accounts, records the visit of the Wise Men rather than that of the shepherds, no doubt as being more in accord with the kingly aspect. Predictably, there is more quoting from the Old Testament in Matthew than in the other Gospels—a great deal of it supporting the Messianic claim. Matthew was probably written some ten or fifteen years later than Mark, which would put it at around C.E. 75–80.

Mark, as we have said, was almost without question the first written, and the date of about C.E. 65, probably after the traditional martyrdom of Peter and Paul under Nero, is well accepted. Along with being the first, Mark is much the shortest. He reminds me of a newspaper reporter. Two of his favorite words are "straightway" and "immediately," for he is concerned with getting on with the story, with recounting what actually happened more than with details of what was said or with the interpretation of events.

Mark comes through as the Gospel of the mighty Son of God, of the wonder-working Servant. He is much concerned with Jesus' power and with the miracles. He omits any description of Jesus' birth and youth, and opens with his ministry preceded by half a dozen verses about John the Baptist. As the other three Gospel writers have done, Mark devotes a seemingly disproportionate amount of space to Passion week. A good example of Mark's abbreviated style is seen in the account of the temptations in the wilderness. Matthew tells the story in eleven verses; Luke uses thirteen; while Mark does it in two. John omits this material entirely.

Luke is the Gospel of beauty and compassion—the Gospel of Jesus, the Savior of all sorts of people. He emphasizes Jesus' love and concern for the dregs of society and for all the disadvantaged, for Samaritans, women, sinners, and the like. There is general agreement that the author of Luke is the "beloved physician" mentioned by Paul, his companion on much of his travel, and the only Gentile writer of Scripture.

The author of Luke is a careful historian, and his Greek, both in Luke and in his second volume, Acts, is the best in the New Testament. Only Luke gives us the one incident we have of Jesus' youth, the visit to the Temple in Jerusalem at the age of twelve, and the beautiful inclusive verse about his growing years: "And Jesus increased in wisdom and stature, and in favor with God and man" (2:52). The author's medical background comes through in his interest in detail in the healing miracles and in his use of language. When Jesus talks about the eye of a needle and the camel, Mark and Matthew use the Greek word for a tailor's needle, but in Luke it is a surgeon's needle. There are numerous other examples.

We would have neither the parable of the good Samaritan nor that of the prodigal son without Luke. And we would lack surely the best-loved Christmas account, beginning, "And there were in the same country shepherds abiding in the field, keeping watch over their flock by night" (2:8). I believe if, perish the thought, I could have only one of the Bible's sixty-six books, it would have to be Luke.

John, as mentioned before, is very different from the other three. There are differing opinions as to its date and author. The most widely accepted opinion is that it was written by, or at least from information received from, John, the brother of James, the son of Zebedee, probably the youngest of the Twelve, toward the end of a long life in probably C.E. 90. John is more concerned with interpretation than are the other three authors. He presents Jesus as the incarnate Word, the eternal Son of God. He spells out his purpose clearly in the last verse of the twentieth chapter: "But these are written, that ye might believe that Jesus is the Christ, the Son of God; and that believing ye might have life through his name" (20:31).

Let us look, then, at the bare bones of the story that these four books tell. Incidentally, a good way to study the Gospels is with a harmony in which the parallel accounts are set up in columns. In Matthew and in Luke, we get the birth stories, already mentioned. Jesus was born in either C.E. 4 or 6 due to a mistake made in the revision of the calendar, which is too bad since this is the watershed of the Bible, indeed of human history!

John does not record the birth of Christ, but opens with the beautiful verses about the incarnate Word—the Word made flesh. From the birth to the beginning of Jesus' ministry some thirty years later, we know nothing except for Luke's interlude. At around C.E. 26, John the Baptist appears to prepare the way, and Christ is baptized by him—reluctantly. Why baptism, the sign of repentance and forgiveness of sin, for one who knew no sin? Well, because he identified with the people he came to save. He accepted John's ministry as being of God and he perhaps felt that in baptism he signified the fact that the kingdom of God was at hand. He may well have felt that his baptism was an act of dedication to his Creator's will and an anointing with power.

Next come the temptations in the wilderness, recorded in all three Synoptics. What is temptation? One scholar, whose name I'm sorry I don't remember, has defined temptation as "an appeal to natural desire, which is basically good, to go beyond the limits set by God." The first temptation was to be an economic Messiah, to turn stones to bread. I do not believe that this temptation was surely just to satisfy Jesus' hunger, but to feed humankind (so many of whom were hungry then as they are now). Jesus did feed people on occasion, but he would not make the material his primary goal.

Then there was the temptation to be a marvelous Messiah, to cast himself down from the pinnacle of the Temple, be miraculously preserved by God's angels, and so to begin his ministry with a large group of adoring followers. Just as he fed the masses, but would not be an economic Messiah, so he performed miracles but would not make them his priority. Jesus always refused to put on a show. All of Jesus' miracles were low-key, played down. The other temptation was to be a political Messiah, to emulate David and to attempt to fulfill the kingdom's purpose by political maneuvering and military force. In other words, to worship power. He would have none of it.

The first part of Jesus' ministry was in Galilee, according to the Synoptics. In John, it appears there was an early period in Judea. I would remind you again that the Bible is not too concerned with chronology. Some time early in his ministry, Jesus preached from Isaiah in the Nazareth synagogue and was rejected by his hometown. After that, Capernaum, on the coast of Galilee, became his base of operations. It was there that he called the first disciples, Peter and Andrew, James and John. He preached, and he taught. He healed all manner of diseases. He cast out demons.

Jesus' fame begins to spread, and before long he is so thronged by the crowds that four friends carrying a paralyzed man are forced to remove a part of the roof of the house where Jesus is speaking in order to get their friend to the feet of the master. Opposition begins. His message is joyous and different, and it cannot be contained in the traditional patterns of Judaism. He chooses the remainder of the Twelve to be with him and to carry out his mission.

An outstanding example of his teachings is found in the Sermon on the Mount. This sermon is, once more to oversimplify, a collection of the things Christ had to say concerning life in the kingdom of God. It is found in Matthew 5, 6, and 7, and a part of it is recorded in Luke 6. These were startling teachings, then, in the intervening centuries, and they are no less startling today: "If thine eye offend thee, pluck it out"; "judge not, that ye be not judged"; "lay not up for yourselves treasures on earth"; "love your enemy, do good to those who hate you"; "blessed are the meek"; "if a man smite thee on one cheek, turn the other"; "take no thought for the morrow." Our gut reaction now, as it must have been then, is NO WAY!! How can we possibly deal with this collection of unrealistic demands?!

Scholars have, with great effort, come up with ways to make these characteristics of the kingdom more palatable. Some say the sayings were intended only for the disciples, who were set apart for a special mission. Some say the teachings are a set of interim ethics set down by those who were convinced that the end of the world and the Second Coming were imminent—figuring, presumably, that it may be possible to live on a high plane as long as it's for a very short period. It has been said that these are impossible ideals set forth to show that, because we are incapable of attaining them, we are consequently convicted of sin. Another possibility, and the one I like best (perhaps because I can come nearer to being comfortable with it) is that these are goals to strive toward—ethics of intention similar to well-known quotations such as "Hitch your wagon to a star."[1] Or

Ah, but a man's reach should exceed his grasp,
Or what's a heaven for?[2]

There is also, of course, the frightening, awesome possibility that these teachings mean exactly what they say—that they were meant to be taken at face value. Certainly there have been rare souls who so understood them: St. Francis, Augustine, and in more modern times, Albert Schweitzer, Sister Teresa of India, and other selfless individuals less well known, who bring to their Christianity a dimension that seems beyond most of us. At any rate, the Sermon on the Mount, as well as the other recorded teachings of the master, needs to be read and reread with a firm (if reluctant) conviction that the nearer we can come to the ideals, the better we will know what Christ meant by the more *abundant life* he came to bring.

---

[1] Quotation attributed to Ralph Waldo Emerson, from "Civilization," "Society and Solitude," in *Bartlett's Familiar Quotations.* Copyright © 1955, 1965, 1968, 1980 by Little, Brown and Company. Boston: Little, Brown and Company, p. 499.

[2] Quotation attributed to Robert Browning, from "Andrea del Sarto," in *Bartlett's Familiar Quotations,* p. 543.

The sermon closes with the magnificent, meaningful parable of the two houses: the one built on sand, the other on a rock. You will remember that identical things happened to both houses; "And the rains descended, and the floods came, and the winds blew, and beat upon that house" (Matt. 7:27). The one with the rock foundation was spared none of the vicissitudes that befell the house with the shifting foundation. The only difference was that the one was able to withstand the tempest while the other was not.

This is all we are really promised. Not that we will be spared the tragedies that are part of life. Only that, if we are Christ's, somehow they will not destroy us. This parable is the perfect answer to "Why did this happen to me?"—the "I've always been a good Christian" question that I mentioned earlier. The house we build is the house we live in. How much it needs a foundation of faith and love and trust!

Jesus' teachings were marvelous, difficult, compelling. His deeds were simple, compassionate, and miraculous. The latter, of course, were in large measure responsible for the rapidity with which his fame grew.

The miracles make a fascinating study. They can be put roughly into three classes: those dealing with nature (turning water into wine at the wedding feast, stilling the storm, walking on the water, the coin in the fish's mouth, the miraculous haul of fish, the feeding of the five thousand, which is, incidentally, the only miracle described in all four Gospels), the three accounts of raising people from the dead (the widow's son at Nain, Jairus's daughter, and Lazarus), and the healing miracles, (the lame, the blind, lepers, the mentally ill, the paralytics, and probably many not specifically mentioned). There is one verse in Mark that says "And he healed many that were sick of divers diseases" (1:34). In my earlier years, I figured they had the bends. On a par with this notion was my vision of a man told to take up his bed and walk staggering down the street under the weight of a brass bed like the one I slept in during my elementary school years!

It is interesting that faith played an important part in many of the miracles, but not in all. Some were apparently performed simply because Jesus could not bear to see suffering and do nothing about it. When faith was involved, it was often the faith of the sufferer. But again, not always, for sometimes it was the faith of friends or a family. There is one example of a miracle performed without Jesus' knowledge or volition. When he was on his way to the house of Jairus to heal his daughter (who was dead by the time he got there), his disciples had to push a way through the crowds for him. A woman, who had suffered from hemorrhaging for more than twelve years and (frankly recorded by Dr. Luke as well as by Mark) "had spent all her living upon physicians, neither could be healed of any" according to Luke 8:43. She crept through the crowd, touched the hem of Jesus' robe, and was made whole because of her faith.

What are we to say about the miracles? If we can accept the miracle of the Incarnation and that of the resurrection, then these should not present a problem. It is very likely that some of Jesus' healing was psychosomatic (we hear more and more today about the interrelation of mind and body, and that a possible 50 percent of all patients have no discernible functional disorder). There are also numerous well-documented instances of healing today that can be classed as miraculous, where patients are given a short time to live and yet recover against all odds. And there are, of course, the widely publicized faith healers not to mention the Christian Science Church. Some ministers and laypersons feel that the twentieth century church has neglected the healing ministry to its discredit. I am somewhat ambivalent here. What I want is a well-educated, well-trained, devout medical doctor! And there are many of them.

Again, in the kind of study that I planned this to be, there is not space for any exhaustive treatment of the healing miracles, nor would I consider myself competent for such a treatment. Certainly there was no doubt in the minds of Jesus' followers, nor of the people in general, as to the reality of what he had been able to do. There was too much evidence: the blind saw, the deaf heard, the lame walked, the lepers were cleansed, and what a commotion that must have caused, when unclean outcasts were restored to their loved ones. Inevitably Jesus' fame grew, until it was almost impossible for him to find any respite from the throngs of people. Some no doubt were simply curious. Some were convinced that he was the Messiah. Some beseeched his help for themselves or for those they loved. Some were drawn by his words and his personality. And as his fame grew, so did the opposition from those who were his enemies. Why, do you wonder? Well, most of his enemies were the religious leaders: the scribes, the Pharisees, the high priest and his adherents. Some were sincere in believing that he was not the Messiah but an imposter, and hence by definition a blasphemer. He challenged traditions and customs that were dear to them. They were jealous of his popularity with the people. They saw him as a threat to their power and authority and also to their pocketbooks, for he denounced extortion and the exorbitant price of sacrifices at the Temple and the money exchange for the temple coinage. This came to a head when he drove the money changers from the temple court in Jerusalem. He cut their consciences by his denunciation of their hypocrisy and mistreatment of the poor. It is always disturbing to wonder what the pillars of our churches today would do if we were confronted by the man of Galilee.

Jesus' opponents accused him of breaking the Sabbath. He and his disciples walked through a field of grain, shaking out the morsels into their hands (this equalled threshing and was forbidden). He healed on the Sabbath and was denounced for such acts of mercy. He did many unorthodox things. He talked to women, even to a Samaritan woman knowing full well that good Jews "have no dealings with the Samaritans" (John 4:9). He ate with tax collectors, who were regarded as traitors. He forgave sins, a prerogative only of Jehovah. He was gentle with harlots and criminals. It is small wonder that the respectable upper crust feared and hated him. Above all, he forced his hearers to look deep into themselves and see their self-centeredness, their lack of compassion and empathy, their evasions of God's will through miniscule observations of some of the Mosaic law, their greed, and their preoccupation with material security. None of this really makes for a comfortable state of mind, and many of the Jews just wanted a comfortable religion. And what about us today? What kind of religion do we want to be a part of?

One day at our church in Memphis, after Gordon had preached a fairly soul-searching sermon on race relations, a member and good friend said to me, "Betty, I wish you'd tell Gordon that I don't come to church to be stirred up and disturbed, I come to be consoled and comforted." My hackles rose, of course. Yet I had to admit that she wasn't entirely wrong. We ought to want to be challenged and shaken up when we come to church. Yet, we are also entitled to expect comfort and consolation. Fortunately, the two do not have to be mutually exclusive. And surely Christ's message does it all.

Who were Jesus' followers? Most of them were the common

people, but not all. There were Nicodemus and Joseph of Arimathea, and rulers of synagogues, and a Roman centurion or two. All classes of society were represented among those early disciples. Why did they follow him? Because they wanted to drink in his words; because he offered hope and relief from the burden that the law had become; because many of them hoped that he was the leader who would break the yoke of Rome and restore the kingdom as it had been in the time of David; because he satisfied a hunger in the hearts of many. The crowds were great, and as they increased so did the hatred of the leaders who finally decided that the only answer was his death. By this time, he has been a public figure for almost three years, and his words and deeds have impinged on the lives of a multitude of people. His closest friends, of course, were the twelve apostles who have spent the most of those three years with him. At one point he asked them who it is that the people believe him to be, and they answered that some think he is John the Baptist returned from the dead (Herod had had him beheaded, you may remember, at the behest of Herodias and her daughter Salome). Others believed that he was one of the prophets. He asked them directly for their declaration, and Peter made it for them all: "Thou art the Christ, the Son of the living God" (Matt. 16:16).

Jesus had spent a great deal of time with these men and had told them many things, some of which they understood and much of which they were yet to comprehend. They were all too aware of the danger Jesus was in, and they tried to persuade him to stay away, but with no success. The record says that Jesus "steadfastly set his face to go to Jerusalem" (Luke 9:51).

And so we move into the events of the last week of Jesus' life. It was obviously considered of paramount importance by the writers of the four Gospels, since in each one it is given a disproportionate amount of space in relation to the time covered. In Matthew, eight out of twenty-eight chapters deal with Holy Week. In Mark, six out of sixteen. In Luke, six of twenty-four. And in John, ten of twenty-one.

On Palm Sunday, we have Jesus' entry into Jerusalem—often called the triumphant entry. And it was. But it was also humble. He rode upon a little donkey rather than a fiery Arab steed or a lordly camel. The humble beast was significant and also a fulfillment of prophecy. Remember that very likely many of those who cried

"Hosanna" on Sunday were among those who shouted "Crucify him" by Friday.

Jesus spent the nights of Passion week in Bethany, with Lazarus and his sisters. He cleansed the Temple, casting out the money changers and those who sold the sacrificial animals, and accusing them of making his Father's house of prayer a den of thieves. You may want to remember this incident when you are inclined to be put off by Jesus' gentleness and meekness. He spent a great deal of time that last week in the Temple, preaching, teaching, being challenged by the elders and chief priests, and both answering their questions and asking ones of his own. One notable example of the traps they set and his skill in evading them was the question about paying taxes to Rome. They asked him whether it was lawful for the Jews to pay tribute to Caesar, figuring that if he said yes he would lose many adherents who bitterly hated the yoke of Rome, while if he said no they would have a basis for accusing him to the Roman officials. His answer, "Render to Caesar the things that are Caesar's, and to God the things that are God's" (Mark 12:17). Of course, this passage can be taken as an indication of a Christian's duty to his or her nation as well as to his or her Creator. At any rate, it left Jesus' enemies with nothing more to say at that point.

Jesus told at this time a number of parables. Parables of warning, of the destruction of Jerusalem, of the end of the world, of the use of one's talents, and of a Christian's responsibility. Perhaps the most notable of these parables is found at the end of the twenty-fifth chapter of Matthew, the parable of the last judgment. Those appearing for judgment are divided into two groups. One group was told to enter into joy and inherit the kingdom prepared for them (v. 34) because: "For I was ahungered, and ye gave me meat: I was thirsty, and ye gave me drink: I was a stranger, and ye took me in: Naked, and ye clothed me: I was sick, and ye visited me: I was in prison, and ye came unto me" (vs. 35-36). They reply in surprise that, while surely they would have done all these things, they never saw Christ in need and so never ministered to him. The answer, "Inasmuch as ye have done *it* unto one of the least of these my brethren, ye have done *it* unto me" (v. 40), is surely a clear support for the social action sphere of the church. It is also a reminder of a fact that came through everything during his ministry—that the only criterion Jesus ever used for giving help was need. This is often hard for us to accept because it seems easier to help those who "deserve" it, who do their best and are in need through no fault of their own. But, I have never been able to dig up any scriptural support for helping people only on that basis. It would be a lot less frustrating if I could!

So Passion week is a crowded week, filled with important teachings, attempts to prepare the apostles for Jesus' death and resurrection, denunciations of hypocrisy, self-centeredness, and greed. Thursday is the night of the Passover feast, and it is prepared for Jesus and the Twelve in an upper room. Meanwhile the leaders of the Jews have bribed Judas Iscariot to let them know when Christ can be taken without causing an uproar among the people. At the Last Supper, Jesus institutes the Christian Communion, the feast of remembrance. He foretells his betrayal by Judas, and Judas leaves. "He then, having received the sop, went immediately out; and it was night" (John 13:30).

And how dark a night! Jesus washes his disciples' feet, in an overpowering example of humility, love, and service. He reiterates his claim. "Ye call me Master and Lord: and ye say well; for *so* I am" (13:13). They sing a hymn together and then go out to the Garden of Gethsemane, when, in a final demonstration of his humanity, he prays that, if it be possible even in this last hour he may still avoid the agony and humiliation that lie ahead. But his prayer ends with what is surely the most difficult of all petitions: "nevertheless, not my will, but thine, be done" (Luke 22:42). How hard it is for us to pray that prayer, and mean it!

Judas with the temple guard appears in the Garden, Judas identifies him to the soldiers by a kiss, Peter draws a sword and cuts off the ear of the servant of the high priest. In his final miracle, Jesus heals the wound. The saddest words follow: "And they all forsook him, and fled" (Mark 14:50).

How difficult it must have been for the Gospel writers to resist the temptation to soften those words! Apparently John and Peter do not go far, for we find them in the courtyard of the high priest's residence while Jesus is being interrogated inside. Peter is accused by a servant of being a follower of the Nazarene. He denies it vehemently as Jesus told him he would, and then he bitterly grieves over his defection. Judas goes back to the elders with the thirty pieces of silver (blood money used to purchase a potter's field) and then kills himself. Why? My own opinion, though I cannot support it from the record, is that Judas never intended Jesus' death. Judas felt that if Jesus were forced into a corner, he would defend himself and use the power which Judas knew he had and so become the sort of ruler Judas wanted. But, his manipulation failed, and he could not face the consequences. Are we ever tempted to try to manipulate the Almighty?

On the morning of Good Friday, Jesus is tried before the full Sanhedrin in formal session. He was falsely condemned on the grounds of blasphemy and treason against Rome, and, since the Jews could not carry out a sentence of death, he was taken before the Roman procurator, Pontius Pilate. Pilate endeavors to talk the people (well stirred up by this time by agents of the elders circulating among the crowd) out of the death sentence, since he is convinced that it is undeserved. He goes as far as he dares without chancing a riot and a threat to his position (there were lots of places worse than Jerusalem where a governor might be sent who could not keep the peace). At last he calls for water for ceremonial cleansing. As far as I know, this is where our phrase "washing one's hands" of a matter had its inception.

It is easy to blame Pilate, but just how far would most of us be prepared to go in a like situation? What about housing for those on welfare? Are we really willing to take an unpopular stand when it is all too likely to bring down the value of our property? The night before, the apostles had been sufficiently unsure of their commitment to say, when Jesus said that one of their number would betray him, "Is it I?" How sure can we really be of our own integrity and devotion? And how we would like to evade responsibility if only a way could be found! Pilate had tried this, too, a little earlier. When he learned that Herod was in town, he had sent Jesus to the half-Jewish regent hoping, presumably, to rid himself of a hot potato. But Herod had sent him back.

And so we come to the Via Dolorosa.[3] Jesus starts out carrying his cross, but he is exhausted by lack of sleep, scourging, and the weight of the sins of the world and his separation from God. He was

---

[3]Jesus' route from Pilate's judgment hall to Golgotha.

crucified—the most shameful form of execution—outside the city on the hill called Golgotha. This was probably either the fourteenth or fifteenth day of Nisan (the month combining March and April) of either C.E. 29 or 30. There are seven utterances from the cross in the Gospel records called the seven last words: three from Luke: "Father, forgive them; for they know not what they do" (23:34); the words to the penitent thief, who asks his remembrance: "Today shalt thou be with me in paradise" (23:43); and "Father, into thy hands I commend my spirit" (23:46). John also has three: "behold thy son! ... Behold thy mother!" (19:26–27) (the arrangements for John's care of his mother); "I thirst" (19:28); and "It is finished" (19:30). Matthew and Mark each record one: "My God, my God, why hast thou forsaken me?" (Matt. 27:46; Mark 15:34).

There is the earthquake, and the tearing apart of the veil of the Temple. There is the testimony of the Roman centurion, "Truly this was the Son of God" (Matt. 27:54; Mark 15:39). He was taken down from the cross and placed in the Garden tomb by Nicodemus and Joseph of Arimathea. He was, in the words of the Apostles' Creed, "crucified, dead, and buried." It looks as if it is all over. The wonderful life, ministry, and teachings of the Galilean have ended on a cross between two thieves. The disciples are terrified and despairing. They are a broken people.

But then comes Easter morning. The tomb is empty, and the world and life for successive generations is changed. I believe with all my heart that the resurrection is a datable historic fact. Anything short of this simply does not explain what happened. All four Gospels tell of the empty tomb and of postresurrection appearances to various witnesses. If the enemies of Christ could have produced a corpse, they would have done so, and Christianity would have ended before it began. If the resurrection had not been unshakably real to those early disciples, we would have heard no more of them after they all forsook him and fled.

There had to be an earth-shattering event to change a Peter, who couldn't stand up to a little maidservant, into the man who would in a few weeks defy the entire Sanhedrin. We cannot explain the resurrection, nor can the critics of Christianity explain it away. It explains the Christian church and validates the claims of Christ. There have been attempts at compromise here: those who say that he was a good man, probably the greatest teacher who ever lived, but nothing more. I do not think that this is a choice open to us.

Logically there are only three possibilities. The greatest man who ever lived would not have claimed to be something he was not. So either Christ was who he said he was, Master and Lord, Son of the Esther, or he was a cheat, liar, and imposter. Or he was mad. As far as I can see, these are the only choices we have.

For Christians, he is the Word Incarnate (see the opening verses of John's Gospel), the promised Messiah, the Anointed One of God, Son of the Father in a unique and special way; he and the Father are one (see John 14:11). He is Lord, Savior, Mediator, head of the church, bringer of the kingdom of God, which he saw as present then within his people but as future in its fulfillment. He was, in his days on earth, fully God and at the same time fully human. As a human he became angry, tired, hungry, and was subject to the same temptations we all face. As God, he transcended temptation and managed always in all situations to do the will of the Father. He bridges the great gulf between a righteous God and God's sinful creatures.

10

The Early Church

When we leave the Gospels behind, we open a new act of the drama. The rest of the New Testament has to do with the Christian church, the men and women who were part of it, its leaders and their differences and difficulties, and its spread from a small Jewish sect to a world religion. And all this occurring in a little more than three decades! Here we find the straightforward narrative account of the founding and growth of the church in the book of Acts. But we also get many insights and highlights relating to its problems and joys from two sets of letters. The first set is a series of epistles written by Paul to churches and to individuals, Romans through Philemon. The second set contains eight more, Hebrews through Jude, written by different individuals to the Christians at large.

Acts was written by the author of Luke and is a sequel to that Gospel. It is a very valuable book, indeed, since without it our knowledge of the early days of the church would be fragmentary and disjointed. The writer begins with a review of the resurrection and the postresurrection appearances with the key verse of the book being Christ's words recorded in Acts 1:8: "ye shall be witnesses unto me both in Jerusalem, and in all Judea, and in Samaria, and unto the uttermost part of the earth." It is worth mentioning that the word *witness* is the same as the word *martyr* in the Greek.

The birthday of the church was the Day of Pentecost, an agricultural festival fifty days after the Passover—or some six and a half weeks after the resurrection. The disciples are gathered together when the gift of the Holy Spirit is bestowed. Jewish pilgrims from various parts of the world are there. Peter preaches a powerful sermon, and three thousand people become converts. The marks of the early church are clearly spelled out: teaching, fellowship, eating together, prayer—and a sharing of one's possessions (the first of many experiments in Christian communism). It is not a success, for by the fifth chapter we find Ananias and Sapphira falsely claiming a grandiose generosity and being drastically punished for their deceit.

But before we move ahead, let's go back to the earlier record— that key verse that is truly significant and impressive in that the witnesses are to start out precisely where they are—in Jerusalem! Then, "and in all Judea," that is, reaching out, but still familiar territory, and then witnesses to Samaria, a part of the country looked down on by good Jews. This had to be a bitter pill for those early followers to swallow. "To the uttermost parts of the earth" may have sounded to them a dream far beyond the possibility of realization. Yet it came true.

Along with the dramatic success of Peter's Pentecostal sermon, we find the curious matter of speaking in tongues, apparently related to the gift of the spirit. No less a great apostle than Paul had his reservations as to just what speaking in tongues meant and how important it was, for he writes "greater *is* he that prophesieth than he that speaketh with tongues" (1 Cor. 14:5, 6, 9). Yet it is a phenomenon that has fascinated various branches of the church.

There is a church in Memphis, large and prosperous, who will not put a teacher on its church school staff unless the individual claims to have the gift of tongues. This was also the occasion for a remark on Peter's part that has always tickled me. Some of the bystanders, on hearing the babel of sound, decided the people were overcome with wine. Peter's defense is surely down to earth: "For these are not drunken, as ye suppose, seeing it is *but* the third hour of the day" (Acts 2:15). In other words, who gets drunk by nine in the morning?

By the third chapter things are moving rapidly. We have Peter and John going to the Temple and being accosted by a lame beggar, who had been crippled since birth. Peter says to him, "Silver and gold have I none [(certainly a usual condition of most of the early followers, as well as many later ones!)]; but such as I have give I thee: In the name of Jesus Christ of Nazareth rise and walk" (3:6). And the lame beggar walks, and the people's amazement opens the way for Peter's second sermon. The miracle, widely broadcasted, also shakes up the Jewish leaders, for whom one can almost feel a little sympathy. They had been sure that when their machinations resulted in Jesus' death, that had been the end of this troublesome sect. To find it alive and well must have been a tremendous shock.

So Peter and John are hauled before the elders of Israel where Peter again proclaims the power of the crucified Christ. Note that this is the same man who six weeks before had sworn three times that he never knew Jesus. Certainly the change in Peter is a mighty witness to the resurrection and to the power of the Holy Spirit, who, incidentally, is one of the main characters in the book of Acts. Some scholars say the book might more appropriately be titled "The Acts of the Holy Spirit." There are forty references to it (him, her?) in the first thirteen chapters.

By the sixth chapter of Acts, there is some minor dissension in the church. The perfect harmony that prevailed in the very early days did not last long. By now (it could have been a year and a half after Pentecost) swiftly in Acts, the church has grown, and there are in it, as today, a number of widows. Perhaps the women were the more durable sex, then as now. They did not, however, have the money that some of our widows have today, and their plight was by and large a difficult one. A claim is made that the widows of the Hebrews are favored over the Grecian ones. And the twelve apostles (or eleven, plus Matthias who replaced Judas) decide that they were meant for things higher than settling disputes among women over the distribution of food. They were probably right, but it was an interesting masculine reaction: "It is not reason that we should leave the word of God, and serve tables" (6:2). No Marthas among them, for sure.

So, we have the first instance of church organization. A board of seven deacons is ordained with the laying on of hands. Of the seven men, only two are remembered: Philip, who while on a preaching tour in the desert of Gaza converts an Ethiopian from the court of Queen Candace by explaining to him some of the Messianic prophecy in Isaiah. And, of course, there is Stephen.

Stephen is a fiery, zealous speaker, who refuses to pull any punches in what he has to say. He does not hesitate to accuse the Jews of the murder of Christ. In a magnificent sermon he begins with Abraham and sums up Old Testament events to the time of Solomon, then concludes with a denunciation of the Jews who refused to listen to the prophets and permitted the crucifixion. Peter so incenses his audience that he is rushed out of the city and stoned to death. There are two notable things about his murder: His final words are very much like his Master's from the cross, "Lord, lay not this sin to their charge" (7:60); and those who did the stoning "laid down their clothes at a young man's feet, whose name was Saul" (v. 58).

This is our introduction to the most important apostle in the early church: Saul who would later be called Paul. He threw none of the stones that rained on Stephen, but he was willing to hold the coats of those who did. I am convinced in my own mind that Saul's conversion began then. No man with his intelligence could watch another man die as Stephen did without wondering about the strength of his faith and not question his own.

As far as external evidence went, Saul simply increased the intensity of his devotion to wiping out the Christians. Have you never seen this in yourself? If you are a bit dubious about a course of action on which you have embarked, in order to stifle your doubts, don't you go at it harder than ever? I am convinced it was so with Saul.

The first third of Acts has the spotlight more on Peter than anyone else. However, the last two thirds of the book find Paul as the main character. However, before Peter takes a lower seat, he performs a notable miracle in raising a woman from the dead: Dorcas at Joppa. Not only was this an astounding event, but the fact that it was a woman is amazing. It is hard for us to realize what Christianity meant to the female part of humanity. Sometimes Paul is railed at because of some of his words about the place of women. What we fail to realize is that he was extremely advanced for his time in history. Jesus, of course, treated women as individuals, one of the charges brought against him. It is worth quoting one of the ritual daily prayers for a Jewish male in the time of Christ and of Paul: "Oh Lord, I thank thee that I am not a Gentile, a slave, or a woman." And in making a quorum of members at a Jewish synagogue, only men could be counted. So the fact that the only explicit account we have of Peter raising a person from the dead concerns a woman is important.

Shortly after this, while Peter is still in Joppa, he has an experience that changes his life and his future mission. He has a dream, or sees a vision, in which all sorts of animals and fowls are spread before him, and a voice tells him to kill and eat of them, indiscriminately. Peter's response is on the smug side, "Not so, Lord; for I have never eaten any thing that is common or unclean" (10:14).

As a good Jew, he has obeyed the dietary laws. The answer is that what God has cleansed, he is not to call unclean. About that time, he receives a message from an Italian centurion, Cornelius, who wants Peter to come and present the Christian message to him and to his friends, a bunch of Gentiles with whom a devout Jew would not keep company. The upshot is that Peter is convinced that the gospel is for Gentiles as well as Jews, and he makes a statement that, from a man raised as a devout Jew, is indeed astounding:"I perceive that God is no respecter of persons: But in every nation he that feareth him, and worketh righteousness, is accepted with him" (10:34-35). Cornelius and his friends are baptized. When Peter gets back to Jerusalem, he is sharply criticized for associating with uncircumcised Gentiles, but he explains and defends his position eloquently.

Meanwhile, Saul has had his Damascus road experience. He is carrying warrants of arrest, signed by the high priest, to use in seizing and bringing back to Jerusalem any of "the way" (one of the early terms for Christianity) that he can run down in Damascus. While he is on the road, not far from his destination, he has a strange and shattering experience. A bright light blinds him, he is struck to the ground, and he hears a voice saying, "Saul, why persecutest thou me?" (9:4). The question Saul asks in return is revealing, "Who art thou, Lord?" (v. 5). This is an indication to me that Saul knew very well where the voice came from, and that, indeed, he had been hearing echoes of it ever since Stephen's death (probably the year before).

So Saul is led by his companions (servants?) into Damascus, where he remains blind for three days and fasts for that period. Sometime during these three days, a man by the name of Ananias (not to be confused with the earlier pseudo-follower of the name) also hears a voice, and it tells him that he is to go to Saul and put his hands upon him so that his blindness may leave him. Ananias has objections, and no wonder, since Saul is notorious for the havoc he has caused in the young church. Yet, God overrules Ananias's fears by telling him that Saul has a significant destiny—to preach Christ to the Gentiles. Ananias obeys God's voice, and when he places his hands on Saul, his sight is restored.

Saul is baptized, and from here on he is as ardent a follower as he was a persecutor. It is three years later, after Saul has spent considerable time in Arabia, presumably in prayer and preparation and after he has returned to Damascus where he has been preaching, when Jewish leaders of that city are ready to kill him. He is let down from the wall of the city in a basket. It is only after this that he finally joins the main body of disciples in Jerusalem—and not without some difficulty. They are understandably suspicious. Barnabas, a disciple who apparently always thinks the best of everyone, is instrumental in getting Saul accepted. The church then enters a comparatively peaceful period, during which it multiplies rapidly.

Sometime during this period there is an upsurge of the movement in Antioch, capital of Syria, and Saul and Barnabas spend more than a year there. It is here that the disciples are first called Christians (little Christs). It is during this time, too, that the first offering for world hunger is reported. There is famine in Jerusalem, and the Antioch church takes up a collection to send to the mother church.

The chronology of Acts is not always clear, and there are disputes about it. However, the period is around c.e. 41, or a little more than a decade since the church began. About then, the short period of freedom from persecution comes to an end, when Herod Agrippa (grandson of Herod the Great) has James, brother of John and one of the Twelve, put to death in order to curry favor with the Jewish leaders. He also has Peter imprisoned, but, presumably because he fears an uproar among the people, does not have him executed. Acts 12:5 reads, "Peter therefore was kept in prison: but prayer was made without ceasing of the church unto God for him."

This triggers one of the funnier incidents in the New Testament. The whole body of disciples is praying for a miracle—that Peter be released. The miracle happens, and he is set free. He makes his way to Mark's home, where a large group of Christians are gathered in prayer. When a girl by the name of Rhoda answers Peter's knock, she is so astounded that she leaves him on the doorstep, rushes in, and tells the disciples that Peter is there. They had been asking this earnestly of God. But what is their response to her? "Thou art mad" (12:15).

How often are our prayers without any expectation of an answer? It is something of a comfort to me that those early followers were also afflicted with the problem of not really expecting anything to happen from prayer!

Paul's First Journey

The first missionary journey takes place about C.E 47. Paul, Barnabas, and John Mark set out from Antioch in Syria, visited the island of Cyprus, and then went up into Asia Minor, stopping at various cities, including a second Antioch in Pisidia. Part of this journey was by sea, part over land. Mark leaves them shortly after the sea journey is over. We are not told why. Mark was young, and it may be that he had anticipated the life of a missionary as being more glamorous than the reality. Or he may have contracted malaria, common in the coastal areas. Or he and Paul may have differed on procedure or on doctrine. Nevertheless Paul and Barnabas continued, preaching to all who would listen and performing an occasional miracle. Their usual procedure was to speak first in the synagogue, providing there was one. If there was no synagogue, or if they were denied access to it, then they would speak in the house of a convert, on the riverbank, the street corner, or whatever. They converted and baptized many, especially Paul. They also aroused bitter opposition. They were cast out of cities. Outside Lystra, Paul was stoned and left for dead. Along with the preaching, they ordained elders in each infant church, and often stayed long enough to see a young congregation on its way. This first journey probably took about two years. They returned to Syrian Antioch, where there was a flourishing group of disciples and an active church, and reported on all that had happened on the journey.

Peter's earlier decision that God's grace was for Gentiles as well as good Jews had met with considerable opposition, which still smoldered. However, it was the influx of more and more Gentile members into the church that precipitated a head-on clash and was the occasion of the Council of Jerusalem, probably in late C.E 49. (I suppose this was the forerunner of the Presbyterian General Assembly, the Methodist Conference, and similar all-church meetings.)

Originally, of course, Christians were converted Jews, with all the Hebrew background of circumcision, dietary laws, and the like. But now the question had arisen: If a non-Jew wished to become a follower of Christ and be baptized, must he do so by the Jewish route? That is, must he be circumcised and follow the Mosaic law? In the case of a woman, must she agree to the circumcision of her male children? To oversimplify, did you have to be a Jew first in order to become a Christian? This was an absolutely crucial decision, and, "there had been much disputing" (Acts 15:7). (Anyone who has listened to the Presbyterian Assembly's debate on the ordination of homosexuals can vividly picture the scene.) Four key men spoke out on the liberal position. First was Peter, urging that they not inflict upon the Gentiles a yoke that the Jews had not been able to bear. Next were Paul and Barnabas, describing their experiences among the Gentiles and their conviction that God had wrought a great work there. Finally there was James, bishop of Jerusalem and brother of Christ, proposing that, except for a few slight compromises, the Gentiles be permitted to come straight into the Christian church. This was a landmark decision. If it had gone the other way, Christianity very likely would have remained a small Jewish sect.

Paul's Second Journey

A short time later (probably some time in C.E 50) we read about the second missionary journey. Paul proposes to Barnabas that they revisit the young churches they had founded. Barnabas agrees, but wants to take Mark along—give him another chance. Paul is adamant that, because Mark had copped out before, he is not to go this time. Neither will give in, and so they split up—Mark and Barnabas sail for Cyprus, and Paul, with a new partner, Silas, heads across land for Asia Minor. They go back to a number of places where Paul had been on the first journey, then head north and come to Troas on the shore of the Aegean Sea. There Paul has a dream or a vision which impels him to cross the sea into Europe. This was the first Christian penetration of that continent. Luke joined them in Troas. We know this only because in the Scripture "they" has changed to "we."

In Philippi, the most important city of the region (in what would now be Bulgaria), the first European convert is made. She was a woman by the name of Lydia. She was apparently a prosperous businesswoman with a large house, where Paul and his companions stayed, and where a new church began. Eventually Paul and Silas are imprisoned because of accusations brought against them by men who had been exploiting a demented young girl, whom Paul had healed. Paul and Silas are flogged and then put into stocks in the inner prison. At midnight they sing and pray. Suddenly there is a great earthquake that causes the prison's foundations to shake, the doors to open, and the bands of the prisoners to become loose. The warden, who is responsible for the prisoners with his own life, sees the turmoil and the open doors and is ready to kill himself. But Paul stays his hand, assuring him that all the prisoners are still there. The jailer is so shaken and impressed that he and his entire household are baptized. This incident, along with the fact that Lydia's entire household was also baptized, is the main support for the baptism of infants by some of the major denominations.

In the morning, the city magistrates send word to the warden that the men may be released. Paul, in a very human display of affronted dignity, says that since the authorities have beaten them unlawfully (because Paul possessed Roman citizenship), the magistrates could come themselves and escort them out of the prison, which they did! They go back to Lydia's home and take their leave of the church there. Apparently Luke stays on in Philippi, no doubt nurturing this young church which was Paul's favorite.

Paul and Silas go on to Thessalonica and spend some weeks there. Eventually, accusations against them are made to the rulers of the city in these significant words: "These that have turned the world upside down are come hither also" (17:6). They move on to Berea, but the Thessalonica accusers follow them there, so Paul goes on to Athens.

On Mars Hill, Paul preaches a magnificent sermon recorded in Acts 17:24–28:

> God that made the world and all things therein, seeing that he is Lord of heaven and earth, dwelleth not in temples made with hands; Neither is worshipped with men's hands, as though he needed any thing, seeing he giveth to all life, and breath, and all things; And hath made of one blood all nations of men for to dwell on all the face of the earth, and hath determined the times before appointed, and the bounds of their habitation; That they should seek the Lord, if haply they might feel after him, and find him, though he be not far from every one of us: For in him we live, and move, and have our being; as certain also of your own poets have said, for we are also his offspring.

Though magnificent, Paul's sermon receives a very lukewarm

reception, along with some ridicule. So, he moves on to Corinth, a large and sophisticated metropolis. Here he spends a year and a half, living with a Jewish couple, Aquila and Priscilla, who are tentmakers, as is Paul. He works along with them, preaching in the synagogue, and later moves to another house, next door to the synagogue. He finally leaves Corinth, goes to Jerusalem for the Passover, and then back to his headquarters at Antioch.

Paul's Third Journey

The third missionary journey begins in either C.E. 53 or 54. Paul passes through the territory of the first two trips, visiting churches he had founded and finally returning to Ephesus, where he makes his longest stay for about three years. This was a large pagan city with a great deal of superstition, astrologers, magicians plying their trade, worshipers of the goddess Diana to whom a magnificent temple has been erected, as well as a stadium, theater, public baths, and library. Paul began his ministry there in the synagogue, but after three months moved to a lecture hall.

Toward the end of the three years the silversmiths became incensed because one of their chief sources of profit, the making of silver shrines and images of Diana, was apparently being threatened by the number of converts Paul was making to a faith in which idols had no part. So one of them, named Demetrius, calls a meeting of his labor union (or whatever). The result is a riot, which is dispersed by the town clerk when he reminds the mob that they are likely to be called to account for the uprising. I mentioned before that Rome took a dim view of any disturbances of the peace among her subject peoples. So Paul leaves and returns to Macedonia, revisiting Philippi, where once again Luke joins the group. They go to Troas on their way home and spend a week there.

On the last night, Paul still has so much to say that he preaches until midnight, to the point where a young man, sitting in the window of an upper room where the crowd was gathered, falls soundly asleep, falls from the window down three flights, and is declared dead. Paul restores him to life. I find it rather endearing that the greatest of the apostles could, on occasion, put his listeners to sleep! I doubt if there are many modern Christians who have never been attacked by drowsiness when the pastor was, like Paul, "long preaching."

When Paul and his companions, continuing their journey back to Jerusalem, reach Miletus, less than forty miles south of Ephesus, Paul asks the elders of Ephesus to come down to meet him there. This may have been a matter of saving time, or he may have feared a repetition of the rioting by the silversmiths. At any rate, the leaders of the Ephesian church come down to Miletus, where Paul makes a brief and moving farewell address.

Most of the remainder of the trip back is by boat. They land at Tyre, above Galilee, going on the next day to Caesarea, where they stay for a while with Philip, one of the seven deacons early ordained. Paul is warned by a prophet that if he goes to Jerusalem he will be arrested. His companions try to dissuade him from going, but to no avail. After some time, a sizable group accompanies him to the Holy City.

False accusations are made against Paul, and once again a mob is ready to put him to death. This time he is rescued by the Romans: The chief captain arrests him, but permits him to speak to the people from the steps leading into the fortress of Antonia. This only inflames the mob further. He is taken into the castle, where he escapes flogging by declaring his Roman citizenship. The next day the captain has his accusers appear, including the high priest. Paul's defense sparks a violent argument between Pharisees and Sadducees, so that the captain, no doubt by now heartily sick of these quarrelsome Hebrews, returns Paul to the castle for safety's sake. Forty of the Jews plot against Paul, vowing to neither eat nor drink until he is dead. There is no record as to whether they did, indeed, waste away.

In the only mention in the Bible of any family, the record says that Paul's nephew hears of the plot and warns his uncle, who sends him to tell of the plot to the chief captain. The captain then sends Paul from Jerusalem to Caesarea under heavy guard to Felix the governor. The letter sent with him from Lysias (the captain) makes it plain that he has found Paul guilty of nothing with which Rome would be concerned. The following week the most rabid of Paul's enemies come down from Jerusalem to Caesarea, and a hearing is held with both Paul and his accusers presenting their cases. Felix makes no decision, keeps Paul, but apparently not in harsh conditions. His friends are allowed to see him and to bring him necessities. Every so often Felix sends for Paul and listens to him. Luke also says that Felix hoped for a bribe from Paul or his friends. So time goes on and for two years Paul is kept in Caesarea. At one time we are told that while Felix listened to Paul's eloquent Christian testimony he trembled and said that when he had "a convenient season" he would hear more about the Way. That word "convenient" troubles me more than a little. There are times when being a working Christian is, by and large, pretty convenient, and other times when it really isn't.

After the two years, Felix is replaced by Porcius Festus, who, early in his reign, goes up to Jerusalem, where, time not having mellowed them in the least, the high priest and Paul's other enemies try to get Festus to send Paul back to Jerusalem. Festus refuses, but offers them their day in court once more, which gives Paul another chance to be heard. Festus then asks him if he would be willing to go back to Jerusalem and stand trial there. Paul refuses and appeals to Caesar his right as a Roman citizen. He has had a vision telling him that he is to go to Rome, and this is his opportunity to get there. Before he leaves, however, there is one more hearing, this time before Herod Agrippa and his wife. Here Paul's defense is perhaps most eloquent of all. The famous words of Agrippa, "Almost thou persuadest me to be a Christian" (26:28), were probably sarcastic—and the King James translation of them is not the best. But it does set up Paul's fervent conclusion that all who hear might be as persuaded of the Christian faith as is he himself.

With the 27th chapter, we come to the trip to Rome, and what a vivid, unforgettable sea story it is! Luke was surely a master narrator, and how fortunate that he was along on this trip. They are late getting started weather-wise, and Paul warns them that it will be dangerous to leave Fair Haven, a harbor off Crete, and roughly halfway to Rome. The captain, however, thinks that he can get at least to the other side of the island, where there is a larger harbor. But they are caught by a violent wind soon after starting out and are at the mercy of a tempest for two full weeks.

Paul can't resist saying "I told you so," but he also says that God has assured him that they will all be saved alive. And so it is. The ship is wrecked, but they all manage to get to land—the island of Malta, where the inhabitants treat them kindly and are much impressed by some of Paul's healing miracles. After three months a ship from

Alexandria, which had wintered in the area, takes them aboard and finally lands them on the coast of Italy, at some distance south of Rome. As they proceed on foot, the news gets ahead of them, and members of the Roman church come out to meet them. At Rome, the centurion delivers the prisoners to the imperial guard. Paul, though always under guard, is permitted to live in a hired house and receive all who come to him. He constantly preached and taught for two whole years under house arrest, and presumably not too onerous, yet with a guard always with him. This is the last that the biblical record tells us of Paul. Acts ends with him still a prisoner and still preaching the good news of Jesus Christ.

Why does the record stop there? No one knows for sure. Some scholars feel that this was a brief Luke wrote to be used in Paul's defense when he came to trial, and so it concludes before the trial. Others believe that Luke had a third volume in mind. There are traditions, of course, that Paul was tried and released in c.e. 61 or 62, that he went to Spain and established churches there and was arrested again. There was a strong belief in the early church that in the great persecution under Nero in July of c.e. 64, after the great fire, when the Christians were made scapegoats, that both Peter and Paul suffered martyrdom then. But that is tradition, not biblical record. With the end of Acts, the chronological narrative of the New Testament comes to an end—and in a sense a fitting one. Paul and Christianity have now reached the heart of the empire, and the faith that began only thirty years earlier with a small group of common people has become a world religion.

Acts is the story of the church. Where did the church come from? From the Jews with their Old Testament heritage, from Christ and his teachings, from the Holy Spirit. Israel was the church of the old covenant, and the promises made to her were claimed by the people of the new covenant. But the Christian church is much more than an outgrowth of Judaism. Jesus, by all that he was and did, brought into being a new community—the church of Jesus Christ. When the Holy Spirit came to stay with Christ's people as never before in guidance, baptism, empowering and witnessing, the church became and remains the fellowship of those who live under the leadership of Christ. At the opening of Acts, a small band of disciples were convinced beyond all doubt that the Messiah had come, that he had been brutally put to death, and that in a tremendous, miraculous outpouring of God's power he had risen from the grave, walked among them, and finally had returned to his primordial place with the Creator. It was these, and those who believed their story, that made Christianity a power to be reckoned with in three short decades.

11

The Pauline Epistles

*(From my Sunday school notes:
The epistles were the wives
of the apostles.)*

We come next in the arrangement of the canon to Paul's letters, and from these we learn much about the man and about the churches he started and yearned over. These are not arranged in the order in which they were written, and probably all of them were written before Luke wrote Acts. Either 1 Thessalonians or Galatians was probably the earliest New Testament book dated probably between C.E. 49 and 52. In a study of no more depth than this, the dates are not all that important, so we will look at them in the order given in the canon.

Romans

Romans comes first, and it is written to a church that Paul did not found. He wrote from Corinth, and at a time when he was surely at the height of his intellectual powers. It is a book best read in a modern translation, and even then it is not easy. However, it is magnificent. The theme is, in essence, that no one is righteous before God and that no one can earn salvation. We are accepted by God as we are because of Christ's sacrifice. We are justified by our faith, not by our works, which are always imperfect and short of what they should be. God has bridged the gulf between God's own righteousness and human's sinfulness by the life, death, and resurrection of Christ. We accept this by faith.

The first eleven chapters of the book contain Paul's assessment of and statement of faith. The last five chapters are largely exhortation to live by our faith in gratitude for what God has done. The grandest verses are surely those that close the eighth chapter: "For I am persuaded that neither death, nor life, nor angels, nor principalities, nor powers, nor things present, nor things to come, Nor height, nor depth, nor any other creature, shall be able to separate us from the love of God, which is in Christ Jesus our Lord" (8:38-39).

One Sunday I asked a group of senior highs to paraphrase this passage and they came up with something like this: "For I am persuaded that neither bad grades, nor fights with my parents, nor not being popular in school, nor acne, nor anything that happens to me now or in the future, will separate me from the love of God which is in Christ Jesus our Lord."

1 and 2 Corinthians

Both 1 and 2 Corinthians were written from Ephesus, probably around C.E. 56. Most scholars think that at least four letters were written to the church in Corinth, perhaps the church most plagued with problems of any of those founded by Paul, but two, or parts of them, have been lost.

Corinth was a large city of perhaps half a million—a cosmopolitan, wealthy port, with a reputation for high living and immorality of various sorts. A large Jewish colony was there, and it was a hard city in which to be a Christian. Paul writes about disunity, adultery, marriage relations, abuse of the Lord's Supper, and other problems that plagued the church. As always, he preached the resurrection:

> And if Christ be not raised, your faith *is* vain; ye are yet in your sins. Then they also which are fallen asleep in Christ are perished. If in this life only we have hope in Christ, we are of all men most miserable.
> BUT now is Christ risen from the dead, *and* become the firstfruits of them that slept" (1 Cor. 15:17-20).

And it is in 1 Corinthians 13 that we find the beautiful love chapter, beginning, "Though I speak with the tongues of men and of angels, and have not charity, . . . I am nothing" (vs. 1-2).

Galatians

The letter to the Galatians was one of the earliest and probably written from Corinth, though some scholars who consider it the first letter think it was written from Antioch. In this letter, Paul warns the churches against legalism and the loss of Christian liberty. He sets forth justification by faith: "But that no man is justified by the law in the sight of God, *it is* evident: for, The just shall live by faith" (3:11). This book has been called the charter of Christian freedom: "Stand fast therefore in the liberty wherewith Christ hath made us free" (5:1).

My favorite quote from Galatians is: "There is neither Jew nor Greek, there is neither bond nor free, there is neither male nor female: for ye are all one in Christ Jesus" (3:28).

Ephesians

Ephesians was written late from Rome while Paul was a prisoner there. It stresses unity, and, as always, the work of faith: "For by grace are ye saved through faith; and that not of yourselves: *it is* the gift of God" (2:8). In his words about unity, he says, "For he is our peace, who hath made both one, and hath broken down the middle wall of partition *between us*" (2:14). This always makes me think of a play called *Construction*. I do not remember the name of the author, but it finds a disparate group of people in an unknown place, where they are surrounded by building materials. Obviously they are expected to construct something. The bulk of the play is dialogue and argument as to what they shall build. The majority vote compels them to build a wall to protect the group from "them out there." Just as they finish, the architect (Christ) comes by with the blueprint. They were supposed to have built a bridge.

Other notable quotes from Ephesians:

"I therefore, the prisoner of the Lord, beseech you that ye walk worthy of the vocation wherewith ye are called" (4:1);

"*There is* one body, and one Spirit, even as ye are called in one hope of your calling; One Lord, one faith, one baptism, One God and Father of all, who *is* above all, and through all, and in you all" (vs. 4–6).

Philippians

Philippians is the least formal of the letters. This was the church closest to Paul's heart and is probably the last written from Rome at least as late as C.E. 62. It is a thank-you letter to his friends, with affectionate greetings and advice, full of the joy to be found in Christ. This is Paul's happiest letter.

There are many prize quotes: "For to me to live *is* Christ, and to die *is* gain" (1:21). And, the beautiful section from chapter two,

> Let this mind be in you, which was also in Christ Jesus: Who, being in the form of God, thought it not robbery to be equal with God: But made himself of no reputation, and took upon him the form of a servant, and was made in the likeness of men: And being found in fashion as a man, he humbled himself, and became obedient unto death, even the death of the cross. Wherefore God also hath highly exalted him, and given him a name which is above every name: That at the name of Jesus every knee should bow, of *things* in heaven, and *things* in earth, and *things* under the earth; And *that* every tongue should confess that Jesus Christ *is* Lord, to the glory of God the Father (2:5–11).

Colossians

Colossians is, like Romans, a letter to a church that Paul has not founded. As far as we know, he never visited Colossae. But he was interested in Christians everywhere and apparently disturbed by attempts on the part of some of the Colossian church members to add to or improve on the apostolic faith by enriching it with elements from pagan practices. He urges that they be steadfast: "AS ye have therefore received Christ Jesus the Lord, *so* walk ye in him: Rooted and built up in him, and stablished in the faith, as ye have been taught, abounding therein with thanksgiving" (2:6–7).

He closes the letter with some down-to-earth advice as to how to live in the world, dealing with family relationships, masters and servants, and the like.

1 and 2 Thessalonians

The two early letters to the church at Thessalonica are not as profound nor as theological as the preceding letters. The one doctrinal matter with which they deal is the question of the Second Coming of Christ, which seems to have been an obsession in this church. Paul warns them that no one knows when this will happen, for "the day of the Lord so cometh as a thief in the night" (1 Thess. 5:2).

1 and 2 Timothy, Titus, and Philemon

The last four letters are to individuals. Two are to Timothy, a young colleague of Paul's from Lystra, and one is to Titus, also a fellow worker; these are known as the pastoral epistles. They are full of good advice for young ministers, both in regard to their personal lives and to church organization—qualifications for church officers, and the like. Ascribing these letters to Paul raises some problems, though not insurmountable ones. A good many modern scholars think they were written later, by a follower of Paul, and perhaps containing Pauline fragments. If we want to hang on to the traditional Pauline authorship, then the easiest way is to postulate that Paul was indeed released from prison after the close of Acts and made another missionary journey. This would explain, for example, the reference in Titus to the churches in Crete. In any case, they often sound much like Paul and are valuable portions of Scripture. The best known verse from the pastorals is, "Study to shew thyself approved unto God, a workman that needeth not to be ashamed, rightly dividing the word of truth" (2 Tim. 2:15).

The last of the Pauline epistles, Philemon, we owe to what Neil calls a happy accident. It is a short private letter to a friend. Paul very likely wrote many private letters, but this is the only one we have. It was apparently sent along with the letter to Colossae, for we read in Colossians 4:9, that he has sent, along with Tychicus, "Onesimus, a faithful and beloved brother, who is *one* of you." It is on behalf of this Onesimus that Paul is writing to Philemon, a citizen of Colossae who had become a Christian under Paul's ministry at Ephesus.

Onesimus, a slave belonging to Philemon, had robbed his master and fled, eventually coming to Rome, to presumably seek out Paul, whom he must have known or at least known about Paul being instrumental in converting his master to Christianity. At any rate, Onesimus becomes a Christian through his contact with Paul in Rome: "I beseech thee for my son Onesimus, whom I have begotten in my bonds" (Phil. 1:10), and Paul sends him back to his master for forgiveness and reinstatement. It is a delightfully human letter, written with skill and tact (both of which Paul could, on occasion, overlook) and a marvelous example of reconciliation on the human level. I think no one reading it can doubt that Philemon did as Paul asked! With these letters our contact with the apostle to the Gentiles comes to an end.

What can we conclude about this man who was responsible in so great a degree for the growth and spread of the young church? Certainly he was a complex character. Intelligent, zealous, at times stubborn and impatient, sometimes long-winded and abstruse in his theology. Yet he was always on fire for Christ and thoroughly convinced of two things: That in the sight of God all human beings were of equal worth—slave, free, male, female, rich, poor, Jew, Gentile; and that faith and the acceptance of God's grace through the resurrected Christ were the answers to the world's need.

I include here a letter that I have had for a long time—and I have no idea who wrote it—but in a humorous way I think it offers some worthwhile insights.

FOREIGN MISSION BOARD
Rev. Saul (Apostle) Paul
Independent Missionary
Corinth, Greece

Dear Mr. Paul:

We recently received an application from you for service under our board. It is our policy to be frank and open with all our applicants. We have made an exhaustive study of your case, and, to be plain, we are appalled.

We are told that you are afflicted with severe eye trouble; this is likely to be an insuperable handicap to an effective ministry. We require 20/20 vision.

Do you think it is seemly for a missionary to do part-time secular work? We hear that you are making tents on the side. In a letter to the church at Philippi, you mentioned that they were the only church supporting you. We wonder why.

Is it true that you have a jail record? Certain brethren report that you did two years' time in Caesarea, and were also imprisoned in Rome.

You made so much trouble for the businessmen at Ephesus that they refer to you as "one who turned the world upside down"! Sensationalism has no place in mission. We also deplore the lurid over-the-wall episode in Damascus. We are shocked at your obvious lack of conciliatory behavior. Diplomatic men are not dragged out of city gates and stoned, nor assaulted by furious mobs. Have you never suspected that gentler words might gain you more friends? I enclose a copy of Dalius Carnegus's book, "How to Win Jews and Influence Greeks."[1]

In one of your letters you refer to yourself as "Paul the Aged." Our new mission policy does not anticipate a surplus of elderly recipients. Also in a recent sermon you said, "God forbid that I should glory in anything save the cross of Christ." It seems to us that you ought also to glory in our heritage, our denominational program, and the unified budget.

Your sermons are much too long for the times. At one place you talked until midnight, and a young man was so sleepy that he fell out of the window and broke his neck. Nobody is saved after the first thirty minutes. "Stand up, speak up, and shut up" is our advice.

Dr. Luke reports that you are thin, frequently sick, and always so agitated over your churches that you sleep poorly and pad around the house praying half the night. A healthy mind in a robust body is our ideal for all applicants.

It hurts me to tell you this, brother Paul, but in all the twenty-five years of my experience I have never heard of a man so opposite to the requirements of our Foreign Mission Board. If we accepted you we would break every rule of modern missionary recruitment practice.

> Sincerely yours,
> J. Flavius Fluffyhead, Sec.
> Foreign Mission Board

---

[1]Parody of *How to Win Friends and Influence People,* by Dale Carnegie and Dorothy Carnegie. Revised Edition. S & S Trade, 1981.

12

The General Letters and Revelation

We do not know who wrote the letter to the Hebrews. The King James Version attributes it to Paul, but as far back as the third century this was questioned. Almost all modern scholars agree that whoever wrote it, it was not Paul. It is very different from Paul's usual style, and there are other reasons for ruling out Pauline authorship.

We do not know, either, to just what group of Hebrews it is addressed. It seems obvious from the text that they were Jewish Christians of fairly long standing, who are now in danger of drifting back into old Jewish ways.

Much of the early part of the book is a powerful sermon on the high priesthood of Christ and the meaning of the atonement. The high point of the book is the magnificent eleventh chapter, with its emphasis on faith and the summing up of all the Old Testament examples of what faith accomplished. He then says that those to whom he writes are immeasurably better off, because we have Christ:

> Wherefore, seeing we also are compassed about with so great a cloud of witnesses, let us lay aside every weight, and the sin which doth so easily beset *us,* and let us run with patience the race that is set before us, Looking unto Jesus the author and finisher of *our* faith; who for the joy that was set before him endured the cross, despising the shame, and is set down at the right hand of the throne of God (Heb. 12:1-2).

The author closes with the great benediction:

> Now the God of peace, that brought again from the dead our Lord Jesus, that great shepherd of the sheep, through the blood of the everlasting covenant, Make you perfect in every good work to do his will, working in you that which is well-pleasing in his sight, through Jesus Christ; to whom *be* glory for ever and ever. Amen (13:20-21).

Whoever wrote it, we are lucky to have it.

James

The next seven letters are named not for the groups to which they are addressed, but for their authors. The first of these (often called "General Epistles") is James. It is not certain who this James was, but a good case can be made for his being James, a brother of Jesus (full brother or a son of Joseph by a former marriage, we don't know), who, while having trouble believing in Christ's divinity before the resurrection, became an influential follower afterward and eventually head or bishop of the Jerusalem church. Against this is the fact that the letter was a long time (fourth century) being accepted into the New Testament canon. And later on, no less a figure than Luther objected to it as "an epistle of straw." Luther saw it as lacking in doctrine and theology. But despite Luther, and regardless of authorship, for most of us it is a rewarding book, practical, down to earth, and with much good advice as to how a Christian should live the daily round.

His major theme is that faith must affect the way the Christian lives, or it is not faith at all. He speaks strongly against gossip, discrimination, against envy and strife and exhorts to charity, patience, and prayer. The five chapters have many notable quotes:

"But be ye doers of the word, and not hearers only, deceiving your own selves" (1:22);

"But wilt thou know, O vain man, that faith without works is dead?" (2:20);

"But the tongue can no man tame; *it is* an unruly evil, full of deadly poison" (3:8);

"Confess *your* faults one to another, and pray one for another, that ye may be healed. The effectual fervent prayer of a righteous man availeth much" (5:16).

1 Peter

First Peter has always been ascribed to the spokesman of the Twelve, though it is certainly possible that the actual writing down, with perhaps some polishing of the big fisherman's Greek, was done by Silvanus (5:12), amanuensis[1] as well as messenger. The date can be

---

[1]One who is employed to copy manuscript or write from dictation.

put at around C.E. 60, a time when persecution was intensifying. Tradition is strong that Peter met his death under the persecution by Nero in C.E. 64. Certainly much of the letter is concerned with encouragement to Christians throughout the empire to stand fast in the face of difficulty and even death. There is also exhortation as to daily living: family life, hospitality, and so on.

Again there are memorable verses:

For all flesh *is* as grass,
and all the glory of man as the flower of grass.
The grass withereth, and the flower thereof falleth away:
But the word of the Lord endureth for ever.
And this is the word which by the gospel is preached unto you
(1:24–25);

"But ye *are* a chosen generation, a royal priesthood, an holy nation, a peculiar people; that ye should shew forth the praises of him who hath called you out of darkness into his marvelous light" (2:9);

"Honour all *men*. Love the brotherhood. Fear God. Honour the king" (2:17);

"For ye were as sheep going astray; but are now returned unto the Shepherd and Bishop of your souls" (2:25);

"But sanctify the Lord God in your hearts: and *be* ready always to *give* an answer to every man that asketh you a reason for the hope that is in you with meekness and fear" (3:15).

2 Peter

Second Peter is generally believed to be the last New Testament book written, probably as late as C.E. 150, and so, of course, could not have been written by the apostle. It is likely an example of the fairly common practice of putting the name of a well-known figure on a manuscript produced by an admirer. This short book warns against false prophets and sins of the flesh. It reminds its readers that no one knows when the day of the Lord is coming.

"But, beloved, be not ignorant of this one thing, that one day *is* with the Lord as a thousand years, and a thousand years as one day. The Lord is not slack concerning his promise, as some men count slackness; but is long suffering to us-ward, not willing that any should perish, but that all should come to repentance" (3:8–9).

1, 2, and 3 John

First, Second, and Third John are generally agreed to be written by the same author, who, if he was not John the apostle, youngest of the Twelve, then he was a disciple of that John. Anyway, he was the same man who wrote the Gospel According to John, because of the definite resemblance in style and content to the Gospel.

First John is a beautiful letter preaching love, purity, and compassion. In a hasty count, I find the word *love* forty-three times in the five brief chapters—and I probably missed a few. Some of my favorites are:

"Beloved, let us love one another: for love is of God; and every one that loveth is born of God, and knoweth God" (4:7).

"If we love one another, God dwelleth in us, and his love is perfected in us" (4:12).

"There is no fear in love; but perfect love casteth out fear" (4:18).

Second John, with thirteen verses, is the shortest New Testament book and seems much like a postscript to 1 John. Third John is written to an individual and is really only a note expressing concern about a lack of hospitality on the part of another church member. Both 2 and 3 John were probably simply attached to 1 John and are certainly of much less value.

Jude

Jude, the last of the general letters, is characterized by Neil as "probably . . . a trumpet-blast from an unknown Church leader to some unspecified congregations around A.D. 100 . . . ."[2] We do not know the author, and it is hard to find the book particularly important. It seems to be concerned, like 2 Peter and some of the other writings, with a heresy that arose in the early church when Christians claimed that as long as they had faith, conduct did not matter.

The catch seems obvious to us. If we love God, then we will try to live the sort of life that Christ lived. But there was a problem in this area in many of the early churches, and several of Paul's letters reflect

---

[2]From *Harper's Bible Commentary,* by William Neil. Copyright © 1962 by Hodder & Stoughton Ltd. New York: Harper & Row, 1962, p. 533.

this. About the only quote from Jude that appeals to modern Christians is the closing benediction:

"NOW unto him that is able to keep you from falling, and to present *you* faultless before the presence of his glory with exceeding joy, To the only wise God our Savior, *be* glory and majesty, dominion and power, both now and ever. Amen" (24, 25).

Revelation

Revelation, the last book of the canon, is certainly for me, and I think for most people, the hardest to understand—and the one I would most like to ignore. A great deal of it I cannot comprehend nor have I ever heard anyone teach it that I thought thoroughly understood it! It is apocalyptic and eschatological (dealing with "last things"), with strange visions, both horrible and beautiful, fantastic creatures, thrones, pits, lakes of fire, and so on. While attending a class on the book, I happened to see the movie *Star Wars* and was struck with some amazing similarities: monsters, peculiar places and beings, and absolute cleavage between good and bad.

A blazing hatred of the Roman Empire permeates Revelation. Christianity was under attack, and apparently the passages about the beast refer to the threat of persecution. Most probably this occurred under the emperor Domitian, a man as insane and as cruel as Nero had been some thirty years earlier. The writer of the book is John, but we have no idea who John was. Though some have ascribed it to the same John who wrote the Gospel, it is hard to imagine two books more dissimilar. If Domitian was on the throne, then the writing would be about C.E. 95, which would not necessarily rule out John the apostle as the author. However, Revelation is totally different from the serenity and love that we find in the Gospel story. This author is convinced that the end of the world is coming soon and that God's enemies will be horribly punished and God's saints suitably rewarded.

Revelation contains two chapters of judgments on seven churches that are about as down to earth as any part of the book. Many of the faults for which the churches are chided could apply as well to churches today: too ready to compromise, smug, halfhearted, lacking in enthusiasm. But most of the book is devoted to visions of catastrophe and punishment, until, toward the end, the visions are of heaven, the new Jerusalem.

Some of the beautiful words in the 21st and 22nd chapters are often used in funeral services:

"And God shall wipe away all tears from their eyes; and there shall be no more death, neither sorrow, nor crying, neither shall there be any more pain: for the former things are passed away" (21:4).

"And there shall be no night there; and they need no candle, neither light of the sun; for the Lord God giveth them light: and they shall reign for ever and ever" (22:5).

"And he said unto me, It is done. I am Alpha and Omega, the beginning and the end. I will give unto him that is athirst of the fountain of the water of life freely" (21:6).

It is a strange book. The nearest thing to it in the Bible is the last half of Daniel, also apocalyptic and eschatological, and also written in a time of persecution (under Antiochus, in 167 B.C.E., most scholars think). Neil says that in the biblical drama, Revelation is the epilogue. While much in it is unclear, one thing does come through. No matter how tense the times and how severe the trials, God is with the people, and the final victory is God's—and theirs.

Final Thoughts

To attempt to encapsulate the Bible—the record of God's dealings with humankind—is certainly brash and presumptuous. But if it convinces a few readers that it is possible for an average, nonscholastically inclined, run-of-the-mill Christian to find material in the Bible that is understandable, readable, and exciting—and, above all, relevant to the life of that Christian here and now—then that is surely all I have hoped for.

About fourteen months before the end of World War II, it was recognized by both the Allies and the Axis that the outcome was inevitable; a turning point had been reached. Yet the fighting went on and on, eighteen months of "mopping up," and a great deal more death and destruction. I once heard a minister say that the same thing happened with Christ—his birth, life, death, and resurrection. These assured the final victory; the turning point came when God sent

Christ Jesus. From then on, the victory is certain, but not yet accomplished. And so our task is to do the best we can in the final "mopping up" stage—always with the confidence that there can be only one final outcome. Happy mopping!

Biblical Chronology

(Most of these dates are approximate only, and many are debatable.)

2000 B.C.E.	Call of Abraham
1700 B.C.E.	Joseph to Egypt
1280 B.C.E.	The Exodus
1250 B.C.E.	Conquest of Canaan under Joshua
1200–1025 B.C.E.	Period of the Judges
1025-931 B.C.E.	The Monarchy—Saul, David, and Solomon
922 B.C.E.	Division of the kingdom
922–721 B.C.E.	Many rulers for both kingdoms; most of them bad
721 B.C.E.	Fall of Samaria. Israel, the Northern Kingdom, falls to Assyria.
587 B.C.E.	Fall of Jerusalem. Judah, the Southern Kingdom, falls to Babylon.
587–538 B.C.E.	The half-century of captivity
538 B.C.E.	Persia conquers Babylon, and Cyrus permits the Jews to return to Jerusalem.
516 B.C.E.	The Jerusalem Temple is rebuilt.
438 B.C.E.	Ezra reestablishes the community of law.
333 B.C.E.	Alexander the Great rules the world, including Palestine.
330–168 B.C.E.	Greek period; then Palestine ruled first by Egypt, then by Syria
166 B.C.E.	The Maccabean revolt and 100 years of freedom for the Jews

63 B.C.E.   Rome under Pompey takes over Palestine.

37 B.C.E.   Rome appoints Herod as governor.

5 B.C.E.   Birth of Christ

C.E. 30   Crucifixion and resurrection

C.E. 50   Council of Jerusalem

C.E. 56–80   Writing of most of the New Testament

C.E. 70   Fall of Jerusalem and destruction of the Temple

Brief Résumé of Books of the Bible

Old Testament

Genesis

"Beginning." 50 chapters; Creation to death of Joseph.

Main Characters: Adam, Eve, Cain, Noah, Abraham and Sarah, Isaac, Jacob, Joseph.

Contents: Creation, the Fall, the Flood, the Tower of Babel, the election of the Patriarchs and their individual stories.

Date, Place: Primeval time, then patriarchs 2000–1500 B.C.E. Mesopotamia, Egypt.

Implications: God the Creator; humankind's sins of disobedience, murder, rebellion, yet God's refusal to give up on God's creation.

Notable Verses: 1:1a "In the beginning God created . . . " 12:3b " . . . in thee shall all families of the earth be blessed."

Exodus

"Going Out." 40 chapters, beginning about three hundred years after the close of Genesis; ending with construction of the Tabernacle in the wilderness.

Main Characters: Moses, Pharaoh, Miriam, Aaron.

Contents: Oppression in Egypt; life of Moses (early); deliverance from Egypt; giving of Law and the covenant; building of the Tabernacle.

Date, Place: About 1360–1278 B.C.E. (Exodus 1280 B.C.E.). Egypt, wilderness of Sinai.

Implications: God's redemptive act of deliverance; God's gift of the covenant and the Law; God's own people, chosen and guided.

Notable Verses: 20:1-17 (Ten Commandments). 34:27b " . . . I have made a covenant with thee and with Israel."

Leviticus

"Pertaining to the Levites" (priestly tribe). 27 chapters.

Main Characters: Same as Exodus.

Contents: Little action and little narrative; this is a detailed code of laws and regulations dealing with worship, food, health, etc.

Date, Place: 1280–1278 B.C.E. The wilderness.

Implications: Rituals of worship and laws of personal holiness spelled out. Sin offering, blood sacrifice foreshadowing atonement?

Notable Verses: 26:3, 4 "If ye walk in my statutes, and keep my commandments, and do them; Then I will give you rain in due season . . . etc." 16:30 " . . . shall *the priest* make an atonement for you . . . from all your sins . . . "

Numbers

Named for the numbering of the people. 36 chapters.

Main Characters: Exodus people again; tribe names, Joshua appears.

Contents: Wilderness wanderings; Aaron's death, conflicts among the Hebrews and with other peoples. Division of land projected.

Date, Place: 1280–1250 B.C.E. Sinai Peninsula; Edom, Moab; to edge of Canaan.

Implications: Over and over the people turn from God, are punished, repent, and are forgiven. This cycle recurs throughout Israel's history.

Notable Verses: 6:24–26 "The LORD bless thee, and keep thee . . . etc."

Deuteronomy

"Second Law." 34 chapters.

Main Characters: Moses, Joshua.

Contents: Moses' farewell address, his death. Repetition (Exodus and Numbers)

Date, Place: 1250 B.C.E. Moab, at the borders of Canaan.

Implications: Moses emphasizes God's goodness to his people and their responsibility to choose God's ways; emphasis on obedience.

Notable Verses: 31:6a "Be strong and of a good courage, fear not ... " 33:27a, "The eternal God *is thy* refuge, And underneath are the everlasting arms ... "

Joshua

Named for Moses' successor. 24 chapters.

Main Characters: Joshua and the younger generation of the Israelites.

Contents: The crossing of the Jordan and the conquest of Canaan; division of the land (e.g., Jericho); death of Joshua.

Date, Place: 1250–1225 B.C.E. (?). The promised land of Canaan.

Implications: The renewal of the covenant at Shechem (ch. 24) and the gift of the land are part of God's mighty acts of redemption.

Notable Verses: 1:5b, 6a " ... I will not fail thee, nor forsake thee. Be strong and of a good courage ... " 24:15, " ... choose you this day whom ye will serve ... but as for me and my house, we will serve the LORD."

Judges

Named for the leaders of the Hebrews after Joshua. 21 chapters.

Main Characters: Many, but especially Barak, Deborah, Gideon, Samson.

Contents: Sporadic (or almost continual fighting; confusion and violence; the people sin, then return to God. Military and religious conflict.

Date, Place: 1225–1050 B.C.E. (?) Canaan.

Implications: Exposure to and conflict with other religions (notably that of Baal) caused difficulties. No central government at this time.

Notable Verses: 2:11, 12. "And the children of Israel did evil in the sight of the Lord ... and followed other gods ... " 21:25 "In those days *there was* no king in Israel: every man did *that which was* right in his own eyes."

Ruth

Named for leading character. 4 chapters.

Main Characters: Ruth, Naomi, Boaz.

Contents: A beautiful account of events occurring during the time of the Judges, in which a Moabitess becomes David's great-grandmother.

Date, Place: 1100 B.C.E. Moab and Bethlehem.

Implications: The Davidic, Messianic line comes through Ruth, who was not a Hebrew. Another indication of the universality of God's plan? (Gen. 12:3b)

Notable Verses: 1:16 " ... Entreat me not to leave thee ... whither thou goest I will go ... thy people *shall be* my people, and thy God my God."

1 Samuel

Named for the last and greatest of the judges. 31 chapters.

Main Characters: Samuel, Saul, Jonathan, David.

Contents: The life of Samuel, who was prophet, priest, judge; Israel established as a monarchy, with Saul as the first king; David's early life; death of Saul and Jonathan.

Date, Place: 1040–990 B.C.E. (?) Canaan.

Implications: "Give us a king that we may be like other nations." Was this one of Israel's basic weaknesses? What about the church today?

Notable Verses: 12:24 "Only fear the Lord, and serve him in truth with all your heart: for consider how great *things* he hath done for you."

2 Samuel

Originally one book with 1 Samuel. 24 chapters.

Main Characters: Many, but notably David, Bathsheba, Nathan, Absalom.

Contents: David's reign; peace, prosperity; David's sin and repentance; revolt led by Absalom; Absalom's death; Messianic line through David.

Date, Place: 1000–970 B.C.E. Canaan.

Implications: This "Man after God's own heart" sinned grievously, repented, and was forgiven. But forgiveness did not remove the consequences of sin. The gift of "the house of David" was one of God's acts of redemption.

Notable Verses: 12:7a " . . . Thou *art* the man." 18:33b "O my son Absalom! my son, my son Absalom! would God I had died for thee, O Absalom, my son, my son!" 24:24 " . . . neither will I offer burnt offerings unto the Lord my God of that which doth cost me nothing . . . "

1 Kings

Named for Israel's rulers. 22 chapters.

Main Characters: Solomon, Rehoboam, Jeroboam, Ahab, Jezebel, Elijah.

Contents: Solomon's reign of prosperity and power; building of the Temple and palace; Solomon's mistakes; his death; division of the kingdom; Elijah's struggles with the prophets of Baal; war with Syria; death of Ahab.

Date, Place: 970–850 B.C.E. Canaan.

Implications: Under God's judgment the kingdom is divided.

Notable Verses: 3:9 "Give therefore thy servant an understanding heart to judge thy people, that I may discern between good and bad . . . " 18:41b " . . . for *there is* a sound of abundance of rain."

2 Kings

Named for Israel's and Judah's rulers. 25 chapters.

Main Characters: Elisha, the widow, Naaman, Joash, Hezekiah, Isaiah.

Contents: The breaking up of both the Northern and the Southern Kingdoms; the Assyrian and Babylonian captivities.

Date, Place: The kingdom was divided in 922 B.C.E. Israel lasted as a kingdom until 721 B.C.E., with nineteen kings—all bad. Final conqueror Assyria. Judah lasted until 587 B.C.E., with nineteen kings, one queen—a few good ones. Conqueror, Babylon.

Implications: Doom and desolation followed the rebellion of the people and their rulers against the ways of Jehovah, with injustice rife in the land. Captivity in a strange country was doubly hard for a people whose faith and whose covenant with God were bound up in a specific land. (Psalm 137)

Notable Verses: 5:15b " . . . Behold, now I know that *there is* no God in all the earth, but in Israel . . . " 17:18 "Therefore the Lord was very angry with Israel, and removed them out of his sight: there was none left but the tribe of Judah only."

1 Chronicles

Named for the type of writing. 29 chapters.

Contents: Solomon as the founder of the Temple; David instrumental in implementing worship at the Temple using psalms.

Date, Place: This book is mainly repetition, covering the same material as 2 Samuel.

Implications: The question arises as to why so much repetition is included in the canon. But as complicated as the history of the Hebrews was during the time covered, perhaps it is a good thing to have the parallel records.

Notable Verses: 29:15 "For we *are* strangers before thee, and sojourners, as *were* all our fathers: our days on earth *are* as a shadow . . . "

2 Chronicles

Named for the type of writing. 36 chapters.

Date, Place: This is largely a recapitulation of events in 1 and 2 Kings,

Solomon's rule, and after his death the record of Judah; very little about Israel.

Implications: Same as above; also the emphasis upon Judah, the Messianic line, to the neglect of Israel, is notable.

Notable Verses: 7:14 "If my people, which are called by my name, shall humble themselves, and pray, and seek my face, and turn from their wicked ways; then will I hear from heaven, and will forgive their sin, and will heal their land."

Ezra

Named for main character. 10 chapters.

Main Characters: Ezra, Cyrus, Zerubbabel, Darius.

Contents: The return of a "remnant" of the Jews to Jerusalem from Babylon; the Temple rebuilt.

Date, Place: 538-517 B.C.E. or 457 B.C.E. Babylon, Jerusalem, and the Arabian Desert between.

Implications: God's gracious act of renewal brings the exiles home.

Notable Verses: 1:1b, 3 " ... the LORD stirred up the spirit of Cyrus king of Persia, that he made a proclamation . . . . Who *is there* among you of all his people? his God be with him, and let him go up to Jerusalem, ... and build the house of the LORD God of Israel ... "

Nehemiah

Named for its chief character; autobiographical in form. 13 chapters.

Main Characters: Artaxerxes, Ezra, Nehemiah.

Contents: Return of Nehemiah from Persia to Jerusalem as governor. Walls rebuilt; social and religious reforms carried out.

Date, Place: Around 445 B.C.E. Much difference of opinion on Ezra and Nehemiah's dates. Persia, Jerusalem.

Implications: Among Nehemiah's reforms was the reestablishment of public reading of the word of God—the Law. Through the returned remnant, the knowledge of the true God was to be preserved and the Messianic promise carried to fruition.

Notable Verses: 4:6 " . . . all the wall was joined together . . . for the people had a mind to work."

Esther

Named for main character. (Persian, "star of the East") 10 chapters.

Main Characters: Esther, Mordecai, Haman.

Contents: A beauty contest makes the Jewess Esther, a queen of Persia. By an act of bravery she saves her people, threatened by the plotter Haman. The Jewish Feast of Purim is first celebrated.

Date, Place: About 478 B.C.E. The Persian court.

Implications: This is the only book of the Bible in which God is not mentioned. Martin Luther felt it should not have been included in the canon. Nevertheless, God's providence is evident.

Notable Verses: 4:14 " . . . who knoweth whether thou art come to the kingdom for *such* a time as this?"

Job

Named for main character. 42 chapters.

Main Characters: God, Satan, Job and his three friends.

Contents: A drama, concerned with the problems of reward and punishment and the suffering of the righteous.

Date, Place: Date uncertain. Uz, in the land of Moab.

Implications: Man does not necessarily suffer in proportion to his sinning. Fellowship with God can transcend suffering.

Notable Verses: 13:15a "Though he slay me, yet will I trust him . . . "
19:25a " . . . I know *that* my Redeemer liveth . . . "

Psalms

"Songs of Praise." 150 chapters.

Main Characters: The writers, David, Solomon, temple musicians.

Contents: Praise, thanksgiving, petition, mourning, Messianic.

Date, Place: Written over many years and referring to many events, from Moses through the captivities.

Implications: Hymnbook of Israel; one of the best-loved books in the Bible. Runs the gamut of man's emotions.

Notable Verse: 150:6 "Let everything that hath breath praise the LORD."

Proverbs

"Wise sayings." 31 chapters.

Main Character: Solomon is credited with writing the majority.

Contents: Practical wisdom, applied religion.

Date, Place: Solomon's reign; Jerusalem. (Final collection time of Hezekiah)

Notable Verses: 28:1 "The wicked flee when no man pursueth: But the righteous are as bold as a lion." 1:7a "The fear of the LORD is the beginning of knowledge ... "

Ecclesiastes

"The Preacher." 12 chapters.

Main Character: The preacher ... possibly Solomon.

Contents: Skepticism, human limitations, weariness, futility—but still a vote for God.

Date, Place: Uncertain. If Solomon was the author, then about 980 B.C.E. in Jerusalem. Possible that it could have been fourth or fifth century B.C., since language and style reflect a later time period.

Implications: There is a great deal of "What's the use ... life is meaningless ..." in Ecclesiastes—but also a great deal of wisdom and beauty.

Notable Verses: 3:1–8 "To every *thing there is* a season ..." etc. 12:7 "Then shall the dust return to the earth as it was: And the spirit shall return unto God who gave it."

Song of Solomon

A love song; also known as the Song of Songs. 8 chapters.

Main Characters: Solomon and his beloved.

Contents: Poetry of great beauty and passion. Sometimes considered allegorical.

Date, Place: Probably written after the exile, named only for Solomon.

Implications: God's blessing on the glory of love between man and woman. Some writers have considered God as the bridegroom, Israel the bride, or Christ the bridegroom and the church the bride. This is reading allegory into it . . . it seems to me without sufficient justification.

Notable Verses: 2:11, 12 "For, lo, the winter is past . . ." etc. 8:6b " . . . love *is* strong as death . . . " 8:7a "Many waters cannot quench love, Neither can the floods drown it."

Isaiah

Named for the greatest of the Old Testament "writing" prophets. 66 chapters.

Main Characters: Isaiah (both of them), several kings (Uzziah, Hezekiah).

Contents: In two sections, chapters 1–39, 40–66; two authors (at least) likely. Most familiar and beautiful words of any Old Testament prophet; most references to the coming Messiah. Stresses the holiness of God.

Date, Place: First portion probably written about 750 B.C.E. Jerusalem; second part during and after the exile.

Implications: Isaiah is the Messianic prophet, and by far the most quoted in the New Testament.

Notable Verses: 2:4b " . . . they shall beat their swords into plowshares, etc." 9:6 "For unto us a child is born . . ." etc.

Jeremiah

"The weeping prophet." 52 chapters.

Main Characters: The prophet Jeremiah, rulers of Judah, the people.

Contents: Impending doom and present tragedy—but also hope.

Date, Place: 626 B.C.E. until after the fall of Jerusalem in 587 B.C.E. Fifty years of prophecy!

Implications: God would not only destroy and overthrow, but would build and plant. A new covenant is promised.

Notable Verses: 8:22a "*Is there* no balm in Gilead . . . " 50:17 "Israel *is* a scattered sheep . . ." etc.

Lamentations

Named for its five poems of lament. 5 chapters.

Main Character: The prophet, the Lord in his anger.

Contents: Cries of heartbreak after the destruction of Jerusalem.

Date, Place: Soon after 587 B.C.E. Jerusalem, Babylon?

Implications: Recognition of God's justice; hope of mercy for the penitent.

Notable Verse: 1:12 "*Is it* nothing to you, all ye that pass by? . . . " etc.

Ezekiel

Named for the priest and reformer carried into exile. 48 chapters.

Main Characters: The prophet Ezekiel, the Lord.

Contents: Visions of the fall and restoration of Jerusalem. Strange vision of wheels.

Date, Place: First period of Babylonian captivity; Babylon.

Implications: A message of hope symbolized by the vision of the return of God's glory to the Temple; the remnant.

Notable Verse: 11:20b " . . . and they shall be my people, and I will be their God."

Daniel

Named for young Jewish captive in Babylon. 12 chapters.

Main Characters: Daniel, Nebuchadnezzar, Belshazzar.

Contents: The first half is an account of Daniel's life in captivity; the second half apocalyptic revelations.

Date, Place: Probably written much later than the events recorded . . . likely last of Old Testament books to be written. The events are placed around 597 B.C.E. in Babylon.

Notable Verse: 6:20c " . . . is thy God, whom thou servest continually, able to deliver thee . . ."

(Note: For the final twelve Old Testament books I am using a shorter form in the interest of brevity. Most of these books are very short . . . though this is not to minimize their importance.)

Hosea

Prophet in Israel shortly before its fall—730 B.C.E.? 14 chapters.

Contents: Israel's unfaithfulness and God's love set in the frame of Hosea's marriage to an adulterous wife. Call to repentance.

Implications: God's yearning love for his unworthy people.

Notable Verse: 6:6a "For I desired mercy, and not sacrifice"

Joel

Prophet in Judah. Time uncertain, early as 800 B.C.E., late as 400 B.C.E. possible. 3 chapters.

Contents: Little known of this man. Judgment and repentance preached; but blessings also promised.

Implications: Written in response to a locust plague; "Day of the Lord" stressed; both judgment and mercy foretold.

Notable Verses: 2:28 " . . . I will pour out my Spirit upon all flesh . . . Your old men shall dream dreams, Your young men shall see visions." 3:10 "Beat your plowshares into swords, And your pruning hooks into spears . . . "

Amos

Prophet born in Judah, but prophesied in Israel, about 786 B.C.E. 9 chapters.

Contents: Condemnation of social injustice and oppression of poor.

Implications: God's righteousness; the social obligations of religion; the futility of "going through the motions" (faith without works is dead?)

Notable Verses: 6:1a "Woe to them *that are* at ease in Zion ... " 5:21, 24 "I hate, I despise your feast days .... But let judgment run down as waters, And righteousness as a mighty stream."

Obadiah

Nothing is really known of this man. Probably written after fall of Jerusalem. Shortest book in the Old Testament. 1 chapter.

Contents: Retribution to be visited upon Edom.

Implications: Intended as comfort for God's disconsolate people.

Notable Verse: 1:3a "The pride of thine heart hath deceived thee."

Jonah

"The Unwilling Missionary." Time uncertain ... probably soon after return from exile. 4 chapters.

Contents: The familiar story of the reluctant prophet to Nineveh.

Implications: History or allegory? In either case, God's love for all men shone forth, and his ability to use unwilling instruments.

Notable Verse: 4:2b " ... for I knew that thou *art* a gracious God, and merciful, slow to anger, and of great kindness ... "

Micah

A prophet to both kingdoms. About 740 B.C.E. 7 chapters.

Contents: Emphasis upon justice, mercy, integrity. Messiah's birthplace foretold.

Implications: God's requirements; love of God and neighbor rather than ritual.

Notable Verses: 6:8 " ... what doth the Lord require of thee, But to do justly, and to love mercy, And to walk humbly with thy God?" 5:2 "But thou, Bethlehem ..." etc.

Nahum

Prophet in Judah, after Israel's fall. 3 chapters.

Contents: An avenging God has destroyed Nineveh, last stronghold of Assyria.

Implications: Old Testament harsh judgment here; hard to reconcile with New Testament thought.

Notable Verse: 1:2b " . . . the LORD will take vengeance on his adversaries, And he reserveth *wrath* for his enemies."

Habakkuk

Prophet in Judah; perhaps around 600 B.C.E.; could be much later. 3 chapters.

Contents: A righteous God punishes sin, but judgment is sometimes slow.

Implications: Some of this book reminds us of Job. There is distress and suffering under a righteous God, but there is salvation through faith, too.

Notable Verse: 1:2a "O LORD, how long shall I cry, And thou wilt not hear!"

Zephaniah

Prophet in Judah, shortly before its fall . . . early reign of Josiah? 3 chapters.

Contents: Gloom and despair; "Day of the Lord" will bring judgment upon Judah.

Implications: After the "Day of the Lord" will eventually come the kingdom of God.

Notable Verse: 3:17a "The LORD thy God in the midst of thee is mighty; He will save . . . "

Haggai

Prophet in Judah, after the captivity, about 520 B.C.E. 2 chapters.

Contents: Encouragement to the people to complete the building of the Temple.

Implications: The postexilic community needed the Temple as a center to strengthen their religious life.

Notable Verse: 2:9a "The glory of this latter house shall be greater than of the former, saith the LORD of hosts."

Zechariah

Prophet in Judah, same period as Haggai. 14 chapters.

Contents: Assurances that God cares for his people and is in their midst.

Implications: The Messianic kingdom is coming.

Notable Verse: 9:9 "Rejoice greatly, O daughter of Zion . . . , thy King cometh . . . Lowly, and riding upon an ass . . . "

Malachi

Prophet in Judah, postexilic . . 450 B.C.E.? 4 chapters.

Contents: The people are called to repent of their sins and their disloyalty to God.

Implications: God's love encourages his people to hope; the "Sun of righteousness" is to come.

Notable Verses: 3:10 "Bring ye all the tithes into the storehouse . . . , And prove me . . . , If I will not . . . pour you out a blessing . . . " 4:2 " . . . Shall the Sun of righteousness arise with healing in his wings . . ."

New Testament

The four Gospels all record the life, ministry, death, and resurrection of Christ. The place of action of all four is Palestine: Galilee, Samaria, Judea, a little of Perea. The time of the recorded events is from 5 B.C.E., the birth of Christ, through probably the spring of 29 C.E., through the crucifixion, resurrection, and forty days of post-resurrection appearances.

Matthew

Author: traditionally Matthew the apostle; at least some of the material collected by him. Date, C.E. 80? 28 chapters.

Notable Contents: Many references to Old Testament prophets; visit of the Wise Men to the infant Jesus; Sermon on the Mount.

Implications: Written for Jews, to show Jesus as the promised Messiah.

Memorable Verse: 28:19 "Go ye therefore, and teach all nations . . . "

Mark

Author: John Mark, nephew of Barnabas, close to Peter. Date, C.E. 60–70. 16 chapters.

Notable Contents: Book of action, much emphasis on miracles.

Implications: Earliest and shortest Gospel; probably written for Gentiles; shows Christ as wonder-worker. Key word, "straightway."

Memorable Verse: 12:17 " . . . Render to Caesar the things . . . "

Luke

Author: Gentile doctor, associate of Paul. Date, C.E. 80? 24 chapters.

Notable Contents: Favorite Christmas story (shepherds); parables of the good Samaritan and the prodigal son; repentant thief on cross. Attention given to birth and growth of John the Baptist.

Implications: This is the beautiful, compassionate Gospel, showing Christ as the Savior of all people . . . the poor, the sinful, the oppressed, and women. Medical emphasis.

Memorable Verse: 12:30–31 " . . . your Father knoweth that ye have need of . . . "

John

Author: John the apostle, youngest of the Twelve. Date, C.E. 90? 21 chapters.

Notable Contents: Ninety percent of this Gospel is not found in the other three. No parables; long discourses; the "I am's (way, truth, good shepherd, light)," "in the beginning was the Word," washing of the disciples' feet; "let not your heart be troubled."

Implications: John interprets as well as records. The Gospel of the divine Son of God, written that humankind may believe in him.

Memorable Verse: 3:16 "For God so loved the world, that he gave ... "

Acts

Author: Luke. Date, later than Luke's Gospel. 28 chapters.

Contents: This is almost our only source of the history of the early church, covering its beginnings of Pentecost, its growth, persecution, and extension. Peter dominates the first third of the book; Paul the last two-thirds. The acts of and belief in the Holy Spirit very important.

Memorable Verse: 10:34-35 " ... God is no respecter of persons .... "

The Pauline Epistles— Romans through Philemon

Author: Paul of Tarsus, the apostle.

Romans

To Christians in Rome whom Paul does not know. From Corinth. 16 chapters.

Date, Purpose: C.E. 58? To set forth his theological position in preparation for his hoped-for visit to Rome.

Contents: Probably the most complete statement of the Christian faith in any one New Testament book. Justification by faith strongly presented.

Memorable Verses: 1:17 " ... The just shall live by faith." 8:38-39 "For I am persuaded ... "

1 Corinthians

To the church in Corinth, founded by Paul in C.E. 51. From Ephesus. 16 chapters.

Date, Purpose: C.E. 56? To warn against disunity, immorality.

Contents: Severe reprimands plus positive emphasis on spiritual gifts; doctrine of resurrection.

Memorable Verses: 13:13 "And now abideth faith, hope, charity . . . but the greatest of these *is* charity." 15:20 "But now is Christ risen . . . "

2 Corinthians

To Corinth again; probably also from Ephesus. 13 chapters.

Date, Purpose: Later than 1 Corinthians. C.E. 57? To defend his authority and the discipline of the church.

Contents: Rebuke, admonition . . . some encouragement. Sometimes called the angry letter. Things had grown worse at Corinth since the first letter.

Memorable Verses: 9:6-7 " . . . God loveth a cheerful giver."

Galatians

To the churches founded on the first missionary journey . . . from Antioch? Corinth? 6 chapters.

Date: Estimated from as early as C.E. 49 to as late as C.E. 58.

Purpose: To warn the Galatian churches against legalism and the loss of Christian liberty.

Contents: Justification by faith; right use of freedom. Often called the charter of Christian liberty.

Memorable Verse: 5:1 "Stand fast therefore in the liberty . . . "

Ephesians

To the church at Ephesus, where Paul spent three years. From Rome. 6 chapters.

Date: Purpose: Probably C.E. 63. To promote the unity of the church.

Contents: Mature doctrine of faith and unity; practical precepts; family life.

Memorable Verses: 4:1-6 " . . . beseech you that ye walk worthy of the vocation wherewith ye are called . . ."

Philippians

To Paul's best-loved church, at Philippi. From Rome. 4 chapters.

Date: C.E. 62–64? Some consider this the last letter.

Purpose: To thank his friends for their help.

Contents: Affectionate greetings and advice; the joy to be found in Christ. This is the happiest letter we have from Paul's hand.

Memorable Verses: 1:21 "For to me to live *is* Christ . . . " 3:13–14 " . . . I press . . . "

Colossians

To the church at Colossae, where Paul had never been. From Rome. 4 chapters.

Date: C.E. 63?

Purpose: To show the sufficiency of Christ.

Contents: Christ is the head of the church, and we are to live in his way.

Memorable Verses: 3:1–2 "If ye then be risen with Christ . . . "

1 Thessalonians

To the church at Thessalonica. From Corinth. 5 chapters.

Date: C.E. 52? If Galatians is not the earliest letter, then this letter probably is.

Purpose: To clear up ideas about the Second Coming.

Contents: Assurance that Christ will come again, but at an unknown time. Advice and exhortations.

Memorable Verses: 5:16–18 "Rejoice evermore. Pray without ceasing . . ."

2 Thessalonians

To same church, from Corinth. 3 chapters.

Date: Shortly after (possibly only weeks) 1 Thessalonians.

Purpose: Similar to 1 Thessalonians.

Contents: Admonitions on work and life regardless of the Second Coming.

Memorable Verses: 1:11–12 "Wherefore also we pray always for you . . . "

1 Timothy

To a young pastor of whom Paul was very fond. From Macedonia? Rome? 6 chapters.

Date: This is tricky, due to a question as to whether this letter, and the two following, were written by Paul himself, or by one of his disciples . . . and also a question as to whether Paul was imprisoned once or twice in Rome. This letter and the two other pastoral letters do not fit into the chronology of Acts. C.E. 66?

Purpose: To advise this young assistant for whom Paul had high hopes.

Contents: Good spiritual and practical advice. Emphasis on church organization.

Memorable Verse: 4:14 "Neglect not the gift that is in thee . . . "

2 Timothy

To same person. From Rome? 4 chapters.

Date: If written by Paul, from a second Roman imprisonment, then this rather than Philippians would be the last letter. C.E. 67? If by a disciple, C.E. 67 would fit.

Purpose: Counsel, encouragement.

Contents: Loving suggestions, advice.

Memorable Verse: 2:15 "Study to show thyself approved . . . "

Titus

To another young assistant of Paul. 3 chapters.

Date: C.E. 65 or 66?

Purpose: To help set things right in Crete. Paul's only contact in Crete was while a prisoner on his way to Rome.

Contents: The qualifications and duties of church leaders.

Memorable Verse: 2:11 "For the grace of God that bringeth salvation . . . "

Philemon

To the owner of a runaway slave, a resident of Colossae. From Rome. 1 chapter.

Date: C.E. 63?

Purpose: To intercede for the converted slave, Onesimus.

Contents: This letter is unique in that it contains no doctrine and deals with no common problems; it is a personal appeal to an old friend on behalf of a new one. Is it included in the canon as a forerunner of the church's quandary over slavery?

Memorable Verse: 16 "Not now as a servant, but above a servant, a brother beloved . . . in the Lord?"

Hebrews

To a small group of conservative Jewish Christians, probably in Rome. 13 chapters. The author is unknown. Some have attributed it to Paul, but the bulk of scholarship is against this. Luther thought it was Apollos; others have said Barnabas.

Date: A time of persecution, probably between C.E. 62 and 70.

Purpose: To encourage Christians to remain steadfast in the face of persecution.

Contents: Reminders of God's faithfulness, traced back through Abraham, also encouragement and practical advice. Emphasis on the priesthood of Christ.

Memorable Verse: 11:1 "Now faith is the . . . evidence . . . " 12:1-2 " . . . let us lay aside . . . "

The next seven letters are often called the General Letters. Unlike the Pauline letters, these are not written to a particular church or person, to deal with a specific situation, but are addressed to the whole church, to all Christian communities, on matters of general interest. They are named for their authors rather than for the addressees.

James

Author: possibly James, the brother of Christ, bishop of Jerusalem. From Jerusalem. 5 chapters.

Date: Has been placed anywhere from C.E. 45 to 60.

Contents: Totally practical advice on the Christian life; social-action proof of faith.

Memorable Verses: 1:22 " . . . be ye doers . . . " 2:20 " . . . faith without works is dead?"

1 Peter

Author: probably Simon Peter.

From Rome. 5 chapters.

Date: C.E. 63 or 64

Contents: In Christ, the fulfillment of Old Testament history, we have a living hope; we must live in accordance with this hope.

Memorable Verse: 2:9 "But ye *are* a chosen generation, a royal priesthood . . . "

2 Peter

Author: probably not Simon Peter mainly because most scholars put the date very late, not before C.E. 100, making this the last New Testament book to be written. It could be as late as C.E. 150. In New Testament times, often a follower or a pupil of a well-known figure would write, embodying what he believed to be the ideas of his teachers, and then would use the teacher's name. This was accepted custom then. Also plagiarism was not frowned upon then. 3 chapters.

Contents: Largely based on the letter of Jude. Warnings against spiritual pride, moral laxity, etc.

Memorable Verse: 3:9 "The Lord is not slack concerning his promise . . . "

1 John, 2 John, 3 John

Author: the writer of the Fourth Gospel . . . probably John the youngest apostle, though some scholars believe it was one of his followers.

Date: About C.E. 95. 1 John has 5 chapters; 2 and 3 John one each. Second John is the shortest biblical book. Probably from Ephesus.

Contents: First John is a beautiful piece of devotional and doctrinal writing, as well as a blast against Gnosticism. Has a great deal to say about light and love. Reminiscent of John's Gospel. Second and Third John are of little importance.

Memorable Verse: 1 John 4:7 "Beloved, let us love one another . . . "

Jude

Author: an unknown church leader most likely, though some scholars think this was another brother of Jesus.

Date: Close to C.E. 100, which makes the possibility of Jesus' brother being the writer unlikely. 1 chapter.

Contents: Warnings, denunciations, against apostasy, false teaching, immorality. Beauty in the final benediction.

Memorable Verses: 24–25 "Now unto him that is able to keep you . . . "

Revelation

The final book of the New Testament, and totally unlike any of the others. If there is a resemblance to be found in any biblical book, it would be to the second half of the apocalyptic part of the Old Testament book of Daniel. Dr. Neil says Revelation is an epilogue to the drama of the Bible, as the first eleven chapters of Genesis are prologue.*

---

*See *Harper's Bible Commentary*, by William Neil. Copyright © 1962 by Hodder & Stoughton Ltd. New York: Harper & Row, 1962, p. 13.